Facebook, the Media and Democracy

Facebook, the Media and Democracy examines Facebook Inc. and the impact that it has had and continues to have on media and democracy around the world.

Drawing on interviews with Facebook users of different kinds and dialogue with politicians, regulators, civil society and media commentators, as well as detailed documentary scrutiny of legislative and regulatory proposals and Facebook's corporate statements, the book presents a comprehensive but clear overview of the current debate around Facebook and the global debate on the regulation of social media in the era of 'surveillance capitalism.' Chapters examine the business and growing institutional power of Facebook as it has unfolded over the fifteen years since its creation, the benefits and meanings that it has provided for its users, its disruptive challenge to the contemporary media environment, its shaping of conversations, and the emerging calls for its further regulation. The book considers Facebook's alleged role in the rise of democratic movements around the world as well as its suggested role in the election of Donald Trump and the UK vote to leave the European Union.

This book argues that Facebook, in some shape or form, is likely to be with us into the foreseeable future and that how we address the societal challenges that it provokes, and the economic system that underpins it, will define how human societies demonstrate their capacity to protect and enhance democracy and ensure that no corporation can set itself above democratic institutions. This is an important research volume for academics and researchers in the areas of media studies, communications, social media and political science.

Leighton Andrews is a professor of practice in Public Service Leadership and Innovation in Cardiff Business School. He was an elected politician, serving in the National Assembly for Wales from 2003 to 2016, and was a Minister in the Welsh Government between 2007 and 2016. He is a former head of Public Affairs for the BBC in London, responsible for the corporation's relationships with the UK and European Parliaments. He is the author of *Wales Says Yes* (1999), *Ministering to Education* (2014) and academic articles on a variety of subjects, including broadcasting policy and technology regulation.

Disruptions: Studies in Digital Journalism
Series editor: Bob Franklin

Disruptions refers to the radical changes provoked by the affordances of digital technologies that occur at a pace and on a scale that disrupts settled understandings and traditional ways of creating value, interacting and communicating both socially and professionally. The consequences for digital journalism involve far reaching changes to business models, professional practices, roles, ethics, products and even challenges to the accepted definitions and understandings of journalism. For Digital Journalism Studies, the field of academic inquiry which explores and examines digital journalism, disruption results in paradigmatic and tectonic shifts in scholarly concerns. It prompts reconsideration of research methods, theoretical analyses and responses (oppositional and consensual) to such changes, which have been described as being akin to 'a moment of mind-blowing uncertainty'.

Routledge's new book series, **Disruptions: Studies in Digital Journalism**, seeks to capture, examine and analyse these moments of exciting and explosive professional and scholarly innovation which characterize developments in the day-to-day practice of journalism in an age of digital media, and which are articulated in the newly emerging academic discipline of Digital Journalism Studies.

Facebook, the Media and Democracy
Big Tech, Small State?
Leighton Andrews

Making NonProfit News
Market Models, Influence and Journalistic Practice
Patrick Ferrucci

For more information, please visit: www.routledge.com/Disruptions/book-series/DISRUPTDIGJOUR

Facebook, the Media and Democracy

Big Tech, Small State?

Leighton Andrews

Routledge
Taylor & Francis Group

LONDON AND NEW YORK

First published 2020 by Routledge

2 Park Square, Milton Park, Abingdon, Oxon OX14 4RN

605 Third Avenue, New York, NY 10017

Routledge is an imprint of the Taylor & Francis Group, an informa business

First issued in paperback 2022

British Library Cataloguing-in-Publication Data
A catalogue record for this book is available from the British Library

Library of Congress Cataloging-in-Publication Data
Names: Andrews, Leighton, author.
Title: Facebook, the media and democracy : big tech, small state? /
    Leighton Andrews.
Description: Milton Park, Abingdon, Oxon ; New York, NY :
    Routledge, 2020. | Series: Disruptions: studies in digital
    Journalism | Includes bibliographical references and index.
Subjects: LCSH: Facebook (Firm)—Influence. | Facebook (Electronic
    resource)—Social aspects.
Classification: LCC HM743.F33 A53 2020 (print) | LCC HM743.F33 (ebook) |
    DDC 302.30285—dc23
LC record available at https://lccn.loc.gov/2019025010
LC ebook record available at https://lccn.loc.gov/2019025011

ISBN: 978-1-138-60897-9 (hbk)
ISBN: 978-1-03-233802-6 (pbk)
DOI: 10.4324/9780429466410

Typeset in Times New Roman
by Apex CoVantage, LLC

Visit the eResources: www.routledge.com/9781138608979

i Cadi a Telyn –

chi'n werth y byd i gyd

Contents

Preface   viii

1   The mounting monopoly   1

2   Silicon values: big tech, small state   11

3   The benefits of Facebook   23

4   The Facebook system   39

5   Facebook and the media   57

6   Facebook and democracy   74

7   Regulating Facebook's dominance   92

    Conclusion: digital gangsters, morally bankrupt
    liars or just serial offenders?   109

    Select bibliography   113
    Index   122

Preface

In early April 2011, Facebook's head of consumer marketing, Randi Zuckerberg, received a phone call from the White House. President Obama would like to do a town hall meeting at Facebook in a couple of weeks' time; could this be set up? After she conferred with colleagues, the event was arranged. It would be broadcast live, and President Obama would be hosted by Randi's brother, Mark, Facebook's CEO. She recalls the event's significance as 'a defining moment' for Facebook.

Mark Zuckerberg dressed up for the occasion. Instead of the trademark grey t-shirt and jeans he normally donned, he wore a suit. President Obama got the first laugh of the day by introducing himself: 'My name is Barack Obama, and I'm the guy who got Mark to wear a jacket and tie'. You can view the video exchange still on YouTube. Zuckerberg, clearly in awe, says, 'I'm kind of nervous; we have the president of the United States here', which was followed by loud cheering from the assembled Facebookers.

Obama was in many ways the Facebook candidate and Facebook president. Disparagingly, Hillary Clinton's pollster Mark Penn had dismissed Obama supporters in November 2007 as 'looking like Facebook', meaning that they were young and inexperienced. Facebook co-founder Chris Hughes was Obama's 'online organizing guru' in the 2008 presidential campaign. Obama Campaign Director David Plouffe now works for the Chan-Zuckerberg Foundation, set up by Mark Zuckerberg and his wife, Priscilla Chan, to distribute their billions to charitable causes. Obama's inauguration was live-broadcast in a joint Facebook-CNN operation compered by Randi Zuckerberg. Subsequently, Chris Cox, Facebook's vice-president of product, told Facebook's monthly all-staff meeting 'this project was Facebook at its best. It was a win for Facebook, a win for CNN, and a win for President Obama'.

In 2016, Obama appeared with Zuckerberg on a Stanford University platform to promote entrepreneurship the day after the United Kingdom voted for Brexit. He said he had that day spoken to UK Prime Minister David Cameron and German Chancellor Angela Merkel, declaring he was confident that the UK exit from the EU 'would be handled in an orderly manner'. Subsequently, the importance of Facebook advertising to the official Vote Leave campaign, confirmed by its director, Dominic Cummings (himself a fan of David Plouffe's campaign skills), became clear. Facebook advertising was also important in the election of Obama's successor, Donald Trump.[1]

This is a book about Facebook. It is not a book about Obama, Trump, Brexit, fake news or Russian disinformation, though all of those will be mentioned. My focus is on Facebook as an institution that shapes our lives, our media, our democracies and our political systems and its role in the development of what Shoshana Zuboff has called 'surveillance capitalism'.[2]

Communication scholars for much of the last thirty years have written extensively about the importance of the public sphere, that space in which political issues are considered, debated, deliberated upon and explored, independently of state machinery and legislative institutions, which Philip Schlesinger rightly says 'is still the primary locus of political communication'.[3]

Over a decade ago, the critical theorist from whose work most thinking on the public sphere originates, Jurgen Habermas, argued that the Internet could only claim 'unequivocal democratic merits' for one particular context: undermining the censorship of authoritarian regimes. In liberal democracies, by contrast, it tended to fragmentation of the public sphere into 'a huge number of isolated issue publics'. Those remarks remain germane to contemporary debates on the role of social media today. As the *New York Times* chief executive, Mark Thompson, has written,

> Democracies cannot remain healthy if citizens do not know what is happening in their communities; if public and private institutions are not held to account and if elections come and go without issues being aired and candidates being scrutinised.[4]

For reasons I will explore in this book, the health of the public sphere is now largely dependent on Facebook (along with Google and YouTube, but that would be another book).

I began thinking and writing about these issues quite late, in November 2016. I had returned to academia in September 2016 after 13 years as an elected politician, eight of these as a government minister in Wales, where I live. I had watched with deepening gloom the UK's vote for Brexit, but like many, I had only become aware of the significance of Facebook's role subsequently, when academics, journalists and activists began to explore Facebook after the shock victory of Donald Trump in the United States. In preparing a lecture on corporate social responsibility for the ethics module taken by our MBA students, I decided to include material on Facebook's corporate social responsibility, contrasting its declared social policies with its role as a transmitter of what was then being called 'fake news'.

One thing puzzled me as I read. I had been the BBC's head of public affairs in the mid-1990s, just as the World Wide Web was taking off and the first Internet browsers were becoming available. I had been present during European debates about the challenges of regulating 'the Internet' and the optimistic expectations that the web would democratise the spread of information and education, allowing millions of new outlets to bloom. But at the same time, I had been heavily involved, on the BBC's behalf, in campaigns to limit the dominance of monopoly gatekeepers in digital broadcasting and to protect European public service broadcasting institutions.

So where, I thought in November 2016, were the campaigns to regulate the digital platforms – the organised collective coalitions of industry, consumer and public campaigns – with concrete legislative proposals, that would be necessary to change political opinion? Fortunately, I didn't have long to wait before signs began to appear in 2017 with angry voices from the advertising sector and the announcement by a former advertising executive, Damian Collins MP, who chaired the UK House of Commons Select Committee on Culture, Media and Sport, of an inquiry into fake news. Meanwhile, a Welsh journalist called Carole Cadwalladr, whom I had first come across in 2007 when I and others were seeking unsuccessfully to stop the closure of the Burberry factory in Treorchy in my Rhondda constituency,[5] had begun to get under the skin of the Internet platforms and the billionaire- and Russian-funded disinformation campaigns in the United States and Europe.

My Facebook learning curve, as I know from conversations with them, has been similar to that of some of the legislators in the UK and elsewhere engaged in in-depth investigations in the period since 2016.

This book commences with my attempt to explore Facebook's developing monopoly. I then locate Facebook in the context of Silicon Valley and its culture of vanity capitalism. Chapter Three examines the benefits of Facebook: why people use it and why they will continue to do so despite campaigns to #deletefacebook. I have drawn on examples from Wales and around the world. A sense of place remains important if we are to address the challenges of the phenomenon we now call surveillance capitalism,[6] understanding that it is pervasive, structuring and internally controlling.

In Chapter 4, I look at Facebook's system, based on its seven 'A's, as I style them: architecture, advertising, accumulation of data, algorithms, attention, addiction and amplification. Chapter Five addresses Facebook's impact upon the media environment. Democracy, human rights and the rule of law and Facebook's interaction with them are considered in Chapter Six. Chapter Seven looks at ways of regulating Facebook under discussion or in operation around the world. Finally, the conclusion explains the fight back against Facebook and its likely prospects.

New developments about Facebook emerge every week. At some point in 2019, the writing had to stop. This will not be the last book about Facebook. I hope that it is timely. Political scientists – I am not one – write about the emergence of a policy window when the 'multiple streams' of the identification of a problem, the development of policy and the right political moment come together. As a former legislator and policy advocate, I have come to believe that regulation is a process, and not an event. The public administration scholar Hugh Heclo wrote in the 1970s that government is not only about the exercise of power but also about the 'puzzle' of policy. To me, that seems particularly true in areas of emerging technologies.[7]

Writing a book is an individual endeavour but the learning that goes into it is collectively achieved. I want to acknowledge at the outset the help of colleagues at Cardiff University. Cardiff Business School has been a collegiate place to develop and test some of these ideas. Other university colleagues have contributed to my thinking. Many of my former BBC colleagues are now in other roles in the media and technology sectors and have assisted with advice at different stages.[8] Some of the themes have been initially explored elsewhere in opinion pieces, conference papers and lectures.

In a review of Siva Vaidhyanathan's compelling 2018 volume on Facebook, *Antisocial Media*, the researcher Robert Gorwa writes of the difficulty of drawing together Facebook research for a single volume account:

> Facebook is just one company, but evaluating it holistically and globally, as *Antisocial Media* aims to do, requires judiciously deploying scholarly tools that represent a polymathic fusion of virtually all the social sciences and a few of the natural sciences as well.[9]

Amen to that. There are thousands of journal articles on Facebook. Additionally, the last two years have seen regulatory and legislative inquiries, and court cases, around the world. Writing this book has required selection.

Hanging around on Twitter has its uses. I have been fortunate to learn more about the themes covered in this book from a variety of academic specialists and technology and media industry executives, as well as legislators at a number of different events and online.

All the mistakes you spot, of course, are mine.

Notes

1 Zuckerberg, R. (2013). Facebook Town Hall with President Obama, Obama White House, 22 April 2011, www.youtube.com/watch?v=3ypVArkbsn8; Brian Stelter, The Facebooker Who Friended Obama, *New York Times*, 7 July 2008;

Samantha Rhodes, Obama, Zuckerberg Promote Entrepreneurship at Stanford, *CNET.com*, 24 June 2016, www.cnet.com/news/obama-zuck-entrepre neurship-stanford-brexit-facebook/; on Vote Leave's Spending on Facebook Advertising, see Dominic Cummings, On the Referendum #22: Some Basic Numbers for the Vote Leave Campaign, 30 January 2017, https://dominic cummings.files.wordpress.com/2017/01/20170130-referendum-22-numbers. pdf; on Dominic Cummings' recognition of David Plouffe's campaigning strengths, see his blogpost On the Referendum #21: Branching Histories of the 2016 Referendum and the 'Frogs Before the Storm', 9 January 2017, https:// dominiccummings.com/2017/01/09/on-the-referendum-21-branching-histories-of-the-2016-referendum-and-the-frogs-before-the-storm-2/; Lois Beckett, Trump Digital Director Says Facebook Helped Win the White House, *Guardian*, 9 October 2017, www.theguardian.com/technology/2017/oct/08/trump-digital-director-brad-parscale-facebook-advertising.

2 Zuboff, 2015, 2019.
3 Schlesinger, P. 2019. What's happening to the public sphere? Communication and Cultural Studies Association Annual Conference (MeCCSA 2019), Stirling, 9–11 January 2019. (Unpublished), http://eprints.gla.ac.uk/181088/.
4 Habermas, 2006: 423, footnote 3. Thompson, M, 2018.
5 Carole Cadwalladr, Burberry checks out, *Observer* magazine, 25 March 2007, 36–43; See Carole Cadwalladr, 'Made in Britain' Still Has Some Value After All, *Observer*, 15 July 2012, www.theguardian.com/commentisfree/2012/jul/16/burberry-china-british-carole-cadwalladr.
6 Zuboff, 2015, 2019.
7 Kingdon, 1984; Heclo, 1974.
8 I particularly want to thank Patricia Galvin, formerly the BBC's Deputy Head of European Affairs and subsequently an executive of Ofcom and the Irish public service broadcaster RTE, whose advice on the European context for these issues was essential in guiding me at an early stage in my thinking.
9 Robert Gorwa, The Last of the Unicorns: Facebook and the Fight for a Better Future, *LA Review of Books*, 4 March 2019, https://lareviewofbooks.org/article/the-last-of-the-unicorns-facebook-and-the-fight-for-a-better-future/#!.

1 The mounting monopoly

I started Facebook, I run it, and I'm responsible for what happens here.
— Mark Zuckerberg, April 2018[1]

Facebook's origin story is well-known. Mark Zuckerberg, who had already successfully developed music suggestion software while at school, arrives at Harvard in the autumn of 2003 and develops software called Course Match, which enabled Harvard students to pick courses based on whoever else might be taking them, and then Facemash, which allowed students to rank others by their objectified attractiveness, involving the collection of photographs from the student yearbooks (facebooks) of Harvard student houses – popular but quickly challenged on grounds of sexism and racism by campus women's organisations.[2]

Thefacebook.com opened for subscribers on 4 February 2004 as a platform for people to post their own content to their own personal profile. People could then 'friend' others to find out what they were doing. Zuckerberg told the Harvard student newspaper, 'there are pretty intensive privacy controls'. Only those with a Harvard.edu email address could join, and students could restrict who could look them up. After a month, it had 10,000 active users, and demand started coming in from universities across the United States to be allowed to join. Zuckerberg and Facebook later had to settle lawsuits relating to Facebook's creation.[3]

Thefacebook.com received its first purchase offer within four months of opening.[4] That summer, Zuckerberg and key Harvard friends rented a house in Palo Alto in California's Silicon Valley, linking up with former Napster entrepreneur Sean Parker, whom Zuckerberg had already met. The social web was getting into gear, with companies focusing less on *webpages* or interests than on *people* and the connections between them. Parker became company president, ensuring it was incorporated in Delaware and ownership of the IP was transferred to it. Zuckerberg had 51% ownership.

By summer's end, the site had 200,000 users in colleges across the United States, and Zuckerberg and others decided not to return to Harvard. According to early employees, 'Domination' was Zuckerberg's favourite toast at company parties.[5]

In the autumn of 2004, Zuckerberg was introduced to former PayPal co-founder Peter Thiel by LinkedIn chief Reid Hoffman (also a former PayPal founder). Thiel loaned the company $500,000 in return for 10.2% of its shares and joined the company board. Hoffman also became an investor. Along with Mark Pincus, owner of Zynga, a gaming company which became an early partner of Facebook, he owned the software patent for sixdegrees.com, important to Facebook's growth.[6]

The Facebook 'Wall' was launched in September 2004, meaning every user now had his or her own 'bulletin board', as well as Facebook Groups, allowing people to organise a group with its own Facebook page. That autumn, a photos feature was added, allowing people to upload pictures from cellphones. Thefacebook.com reached one million users by the end of November 2004.

The company bought the web address Facebook.com, officially became Facebook on 20 September 2005, with a re-designed logo and streamlined typeface, and had 5 million users a month later. It agreed to investment from the venture capital company Accel for 10% of shares and in due course was the subject of purchase offers, which it resisted. There was an early secondary market in Facebook shares. Marc Andreessen, co-founder of the Internet browser Netscape, became an adviser to Zuckerberg and a few years later joined the board.[7]

The News Feed is what today most people think of as Facebook. This algorithmically sorts the material posted by Facebook users' friends into an orderly reverse chronological trail of information, using algorithms to identify the material likely to be of most interest to them. This means each user has a different homepage. News Feed was accompanied by what was initially called Mini-Feed, which showed what had recently changed in a user's own profile, such as status updates, relationship changes and so on, and what content they had added, such as photographs.[8]

News Feed came into operation on 5 September 2006. Data showed that people were spending more time on Facebook than before. But soon, 10 percent of Facebook's users were protesting about it. Some felt that it was creepy, turning them and their friends into stalkers. Although nothing would be visible to people who couldn't have seen it before News Feed was created, the protests continued and Zuckerberg agreed to changes in privacy controls which allowed users to restrict what could be seen. Zuckerberg admitted, 'We really messed this one up', and apologised. His approach – denial of a problem, reluctant acceptance, change of position, and then apology – would be repeated on other issues subsequently over the years.[9]

By the end of September 2006, anyone could join Facebook – 'open registration' – and within weeks, Facebook had 10 million users. With open registration also came a facility to allow users to import their email contacts into Facebook. From its earliest days, Zuckerberg conceived of Facebook as a platform, meaning that it would essentially be an operating system on which other applications could build. The notion of 'platform' also allows the positioning of Facebook as separate from the media sector. For Zuckerberg, the strength of Facebook was 'the social graph', the interconnections and relationships between Facebook users. Facebook was building a network composed of nodes with data flowing between them.[10]

Facebook launched as a platform on which developers could build from August 2006, and in May 2007, at Facebook's first ever developers' conference, known as f8, Zuckerberg announced he was opening Facebook's Application Programme Interface (API) to app developers. Their apps would operate within Facebook, ensuring users' attention was enclosed within Facebook's walled garden. The new Facebook Platform development tool allowed significant growth for developers, as every time their app was downloaded by a user, this would be announced on the News Feed, and they would not be charged rental for their space. Developers could charge for their apps or collect advertising revenue from them. How app developers applied Facebook user data was a risk however – and arguably led to the Cambridge Analytica scandal in 2018, which exposed Facebook's loose data practices to the world.[11]

From the beginning, Facebook's founder has kept a close eye on competitors. MySpace was the largest social network in the world until Facebook overtook it in 2009. The launch of Google Plus in 2011, integrated with Gmail and YouTube, looked like a clear attempt to copy Facebook. Zuckerberg declared a Facebook 'Lockdown', calling all staff to a meeting where he spoke passionately about the competition with Google.[12]

Sponsored company pages started in November 2007. Users could become fans of these pages, and announcements to that effect would show up in the News Feed. Alongside that development, Facebook also introduced a new service called Beacon, which allowed forty-four companies initially to announce in Facebook users' News Feed products which users had bought on these companies' websites, even if the user was logged out of Facebook. Facebook faced another crisis of trust from its users, which this time resulted in lawsuits and complaints to the Federal Trade Commission (FTC) over the misuse of user data.

Zuckerberg's reaction again followed the cycle of denial, acceptance, change and apology. He took three weeks to react to the protests, before posting a statement on his Facebook Wall, 'Thoughts on Beacon':

> We've made a lot of mistakes building this feature, but we've made even more with how we've handled them. We simply did a bad job with this release, and I apologize for it.

Beacon was changed to opt-in. In 2008, Facebook launched a product similar to Beacon called Facebook Connect, which avoided the problems of Beacon, allowing users more control. This subsequently became Facebook Log-in. In 2009, Facebook closed Beacon following a class action suit. The Beacon fiasco led directly to the hiring of Sheryl Sandberg, introduced to Zuckerberg by long-term Silicon Valley investor Roger McNamee,[13] as chief operating officer. Sandberg, a former head of Google's advertisement business, transformed Facebook's approach to advertising revenues.

In 2012, Facebook went public. In the run-up to its IPO (initial public offering), Facebook bought the photo-sharing company Instagram for $1 billion. It has recently been valued at $100 billion. Facebook saw a growth curve for Instagram not unlike that of its own in its early days. The decision to allow Instagram to stay as a standalone app and keep its own branding was also significant: previously, Facebook had preferred to maintain a single brand.[14]

At the time of its IPO, Facebook had 850 million users. In the prospectus filed with its original IPO form on 1 February 2012, there was a letter to potential investors from Mark Zuckerberg. The letter began 'Facebook was not originally created to be a company. It was built to accomplish a social mission – to make the world more open and connected'.

Unusually, when Facebook went public on 18 May, the ringing of the NASDAQ bell by Zuckerberg took place in Facebook's headquarters, rather than in New York, an indication of the company's power. The outcome of the IPO was controversial. Facebook had lost advertising from General Motors, raising questions about the advertising model. Facebook amended its prospectus just over a week before the IPO, to say that mobile numbers were growing more rapidly than the rate of advertising revenues. Smaller investors were to feel that they had not been adequately informed of concerns over future growth, leading to legal action eventually settled in 2018 for $35 million.[15]

Then most users were accessing Facebook on desktop or laptop computers. Today, the bulk of access and 93% of its revenues come from mobile devices. Its mobile advertising revenue has increased from $470 million in 2012 to $50 billion in 2018. Along with Google, Facebook dominates global digital advertising revenue. Facebook's acquisition of Instagram deepened its engagement with mobile, as did its partnership with the games company Zynga, its purchase of WhatsApp and its development of Messenger as a standalone app.[16]

Facebook acquired WhatsApp for $19 billion on 6 October 2014. Whats-App is a cross-platform communication medium allowing its billion-plus users to exchange unlimited text and multimedia without paying for SMS services.

At the end of 2018, 2.7 billion people were using Instagram, WhatsApp, Facebook or Messenger every month, and more than 2 billion were using them every day. Average revenue per user (ARPU) varied by territory: US and Canada users averaged $34.86, European users $10.98, Asia-Pacific $2.96 and the 'Rest of the World' $2.11. Facebook headcount at the end of 2018 was 35,587 compared to around 3,000 at the time of the IPO in 2012.[17]

Economists explain Facebook's rapid growth as being due to network effects: the more people who are part of the network, the more valuable it becomes. They argue that there is a tendency for the leading applications in particular areas, such as search and social media, to attain dominant positions which are hard to overcome: the market becomes inflexible, and lock-in occurs.[18]

Legal scholar Timothy Wu has written that 'when a dominant firm buys its nascent challenger, alarm bells are supposed to ring'. He points out that the analysis of Facebook's purchase of Instagram by the US regulator, the FTC, remains secret, but the analysis undertaken by the UK's then competition authority, the Office of Fair Trading (OFT), is available. The OFT concluded that Facebook only had a limited photographic-sharing business, and Instagram had little advertising, so they were not competitors. Strangely, the combination of data that the deal allowed did not feature to any degree.[19]

Facebook's acquisition of WhatsApp did receive scrutiny in the European Union. In 2017, the European Union fined Facebook $110 million for breaking commitments regarding data-sharing between WhatsApp and Facebook. Legal scholars Maurice Stucke and Allen Grunes note that while the FTC's judgements on the acquisition remain secret, the FTC director of Consumer Protection did warn Facebook that they must not use data on the WhatsApp users. The FTC letter makes references to promises by Facebook that WhatsApp's approach to privacy will not change and warns that changes could breach its 2012 consent order.[20] Stucke and Grunes argue that some potential competition issues related to the competition implications of data accumulation were missed by the European Commission. The adtech entrepreneur and legal scholar Dina Srinavasan argues that Facebook's eclipse of competition spurred it to compel users to accept tracking across the entire web from 2014 onwards.[21]

For competition theorists, dominant monopolies can swallow the markets of smaller insurgents by aping their products. Wu says that Facebook 'cloned' so many of Snapchat's products that it became 'a running joke'. Snapchat rebuffed a $3 billion purchase offer from Facebook. Twitter's success also drove changes within Facebook, in relation to sharing of content, the use of hashtags and the creation of Trending Topics.[22]

Facebook bought the virtual private network app (VPN) Onavo in 2013. A VPN app allows users to hide their web activity. In August 2018, Apple forced Onavo's removal from its app store on the grounds that it violated Apple's terms and conditions and then removed Facebook's research app in January 2019. Onavo collected data on the usage of other apps. This allowed Facebook to decide which companies were doing well and might be acquired or should be shut down as a threat. As Stucke and Grunes write, 'it is as if the monopoly invented a radar system to monitor in real-time the competitive portals'.[23]

The House of Commons DCMS Select Committee released emails in 2018 and 2019 that had been under seal in a California court considering a case brought against Facebook by the company Six4Three. The emails show that Facebook decided to prevent Vine, Twitter's video service, from continuing to have access to its application programme interface. The committee said, 'it is clear that Mark Zuckerberg personally approved the decision to deny access to data for Vine'. Further emails surfaced in April 2019 – Facebook claims they tell only part of the story.[24]

In January 2019, Facebook announced the integration of the back-ends of Facebook, WhatsApp and Instagram. Stitching the apps together would make it even more likely that users stayed within Facebook's ecosystem. On 6 March 2019, Mark Zuckerberg announced his 'privacy-focused vision for social networking'. The fastest-growing areas of social networking were 'private messaging, ephemeral stories and small groups'. While Instagram and Facebook had operated as 'the digital equivalent of a town square', people increasingly wanted to connect 'in the digital equivalent of the living room'. Facebook's new principles would be private interactions, encryption, reducing permanence of posts, safety, interoperability and secure data storage.

This 'privacy pivot' has been the subject of considerable discussion. It was seen as a way of making regulatory break-up more difficult. An encrypted environment in which Facebook did not know what people were exchanging would also diminish the risk that Facebook would be held accountable for what kind of information was being exchanged on its services, whether that was Russian disinformation, terrorist messaging or child abuse imagery.

Facebook isn't stepping away from its existing services. But the new move will allow it to develop its business in a different way, building a private e-commerce business on the WhatsApp platform, using the Chinese app Wechat as its basic model. The key paragraph in Zuckerberg's statement might well be this:

> We plan to build this the way we've developed WhatsApp: focus on the most fundamental and private use case – messaging – make it as secure as possible, and then build more ways for people to interact on top of that, including calls, video chats, groups, stories, businesses, payments, commerce, and ultimately a platform for many other kinds of private services.

Facebook could also use metadata to refine its targeting of advertisements.[25]

Already, criticisms are emerging that the Facebook/Google duopoly dominance is killing Silicon Valley's prized goal of 'innovation' in a variety of areas from apps to advertising technology.[26] Facebook is moving into a number of areas, including blockchain, artificial intelligence, virtual and augmented reality, e-commerce, sports content, its own currency, banking and dating.[27] Competition researchers note how monopoly activity in one domain can provide the cross-funding for moves into other domains. Facebook is no longer just Facebook.

Notes

1 From his evidence to the Senate, 10 April 2018.
2 On technology company 'origin stories', see Wu, 2012, 17–32; Borins and Herst, 2018, 13–22; Aaron Sorkin's film, *The Social Network*, directed by David Fincher, is based on Mezrich, 2009. On Zuckerberg's early instant message to a friend that those giving him their data for free were 'dumb fucks', see Nicholas Carlson, 'Embarrassing and Damaging' Zuckerberg IMs Confirmed by Zuckerberg, The New Yorker, *Business Insider*, 13 September 2010, www.businessinsider.com/embarrassing-and-damaging-zuckerberg-ims-con firmed-by-zuckerberg-the-new-yorker-2010-9?r=US&IR=T; Aaron Greenspan, My Response to Chris Hughes, 9 May 2019, www.aarongreenspan.com/writing/20190509/my-response-to-chris-hughes/.
3 Alan J. Tabak, Hundreds Register for New Facebook Website, *The Harvard Crimson*, 9 February 2004, www.thecrimson.com/article/2004/2/9/hundreds-register-for-new-facebook-website/. On Zuckerberg's early Harvard days and the beginnings of Facebook, Kirkpatrick, 2011, 19–35. The lawsuit with the Winklevoss brothers is well known: Eric Eldon, Winklevoss Twins Made $65 Million on Facebook 'copycat' Settlement, *Venturebeat*, 10 February 2009, https://venturebeat.com/2009/02/10/winklevoss-twins-made-65-million-on-facebook-copycat-settlement/. Aaron Greenspan, whose housesystem site, to which Zuckerberg belonged, contained a section called 'The Universal Facebook', also settled with Facebook in 2009; Facebook announces settlement with another former Zuckerberg classmate, *Adweek*, 22 May 2009,

www.adweek.com/digital/facebook-announces-settlement-of-legal-dispute-with-another-former-zuckerberg-classmate/; and Zuckerberg also had to settle with co-founder Eduardo Saverin: Nicholas Carlson, Exclusive: Here's the Email Zuckerberg Sent to Cut His Co-Founder Out of Facebook, *Business Insider*, 15 May 2012, www.businessinsider.com/exclusive-heres-the-email-zuckerberg-sent-to-cut-his-cofounder-out-of-facebook-2012-5?r=US&IR=T.

4 Kirkpatrick, 2011: 41.

5 Adam Fisher, 'Sex, Beer and Coding: Inside Facebook's Wild Early Days in Palo Alto', *Wired*, 10 July 2018, www.wired.com/story/sex-beer-and-coding-inside-facebooks-wild-early-days/.

6 On the early days of Facebook in California, see Kirkpatrick, 2011; Losse, 2012; Zuckerberg, R. 2012; on the 'Paypal Mafia', see Chang, 2018; Thiel and Masters, 2014; on the development of investment in Facebook, see Kirkpatrick, 2011: 45–92.

7 See McNamee (2019) on advising Zuckerberg to turn down Yahoo's bid. On private share sales, see Lou Kerner, Facebook's EPIC Run Comes to an End, 31 January 2018, https://medium.com/crypto-oracle/facebooks-epic-run-comes-to-an-end-442dee72401c and Facebook – the World's Dominant Media Company, 28 February 2010, http://loukerner.tumblr.com; Losse (2012: 193) discusses how Facebook employees were encouraged to sell shares to the Russian company Digital Sky Technologies.

8 Farhad Manjoo, Can Facebook Fix Its Own Worst Bug? 25 April 2017, www.nytimes.com/2017/04/25/magazine/can-facebook-fix-its-own-worst-bug.html; On the development of News Feed, see Kirkpatrick, 180–189, and Fisher, op. cit.

9 On the News Feed protests, Kirkpatrick 189–192, and Mark Zuckerberg's 'Open Letter' Post, www.facebook.com/notes/facebook/an-open-letter-from-mark-zuckerberg/2208562130; on Zuckerberg's apologies, see Zeynep Tufekci, Why Zuckerberg's 14-Year Apology Tour Hasn't Fixed Facebook, *Wired*, 16 April 2018, www.wired.com/story/why-zuckerberg-15-year-apology-tour-hasnt-fixed-facebook/.

10 Adam Fisher op. cit.

11 Fred Vogelman, How Mark Zuckerberg Turned Facebook into the World's Hottest Platform, *Wired*, 6 September 2007, www.wired.com/2007/09/ff-facebook/. On Facebook's 2007 message for platform developers, see www.facebook.com/notes/facebook/platform-is-here/2437282130; on the background to the development of Facebook Platform and its roll-out, Kirkpatrick, 2011: 215–234; on the link between Facebook Platform and the Cambridge Analytica scandal, see Elizabeth Dwoskin and Tony Romm, *Washington Post*, 19 March 2018, www.washingtonpost.com/business/economy/facebooks-rules-for-accessing-user-data-lured-more-than-just-cambridge-analytica/2018/03/19/31f6979c-658e-43d6-a71f-afdd8bf1308b_story.html?utm_term=.66005e078404.

12 On the Facebook Lockdown, see Martinez, 2016: 288–290. When the head of Google Plus left Google in 2014 and Google Plus was incorporated into Google's Android operating system, Facebook believed that they had won this war – see Martinez: 493.

13 Mark Zuckerberg, Thoughts on Beacon, www.facebook.com/notes/facebook/thoughts-on-beacon/7584397130. On the closing of Beacon, van Dijck, 2013: 48; on the hiring of Sandberg, Kirkpatrick, 251–254, McNamee, 2019: 61.

14 On Zuckerberg's decision to go public, Shayndi Raice, Facebook Sets Historic IPO, *Wall Street Journal*, 2 February, 2012; Lev Grossman, Mark Zuckerberg, *Time Magazine*, 15 December 2010, https://content.time.com/time/specials/

packages/article/0,28804,2036683_2037183_2037185,00.html; Martinez, 5; Kirkpatrick, 154; see also Facebook Buys Instagram in $1 Billion Deal, Turns Budding Rival into a Standalone Photo App, *Techcrunch*, https://techcrunch. com/2012/04/09/facebook-to-acquire-instagram-for-1-billion/; on Instagram's user growth curve, Martinez, 490; Jamie Condliffe, 2018: Instagram Now Looks Like a Bargain, *New York Times*, 27 June, www.nytimes.com/2018/06/27/busi ness/dealbook/instagram-facebook.html.

15 On the ringing of the bell, Martinez, 410; on IPO, Martinez, 417–419; see online bibilography: Krigman and Jeffus, 2016.

16 Goggin, 2014.

17 All current figures and ARPU from Facebook Q4 2018 Earnings, 30 January 2019, https://investor.fb.com/investor-events/event-details/2019/Facebook-Q4-2018-Earnings/default.aspx.

18 For an interesting discussion, see James Currier, Network effects predict the future of Facebook, NfX, nd, www.nfx.com/post/network-effects-facebook; Barwise, 2018; Barwise and Watkins, 2018; Hindman, 2018.

19 Wu, 2018: 122; OFT, 2012.

20 Stucke and Grunes, 2016; EC, 2017; FTC letter to Facebook and Instagram, 10 April 2014, www.ftc.gov/system/files/documents/public_statements/297701/ 140410facebookwhatappltr.pdf.

21 Stucke and Grunes, 2016; Srinavasan, 2019.

22 Wu, 2018: 125; Gallagher, 2018; Frick, 2017, 'Can Snapchat Survive if Facebook copies all its best features?', *Harvard Business Review*, 12 May, https:// hbr.org/2017/05/can-snapchat-survive-if-facebook-copies-all-its-best-features; Alex Kantrowicz, How the 2016 Election Blew Up in Facebook's Face, *Buzzfeed*, 21 November 2016, www.buzzfeednews.com/article/alexkantrowitz/2016-election-blew-up-in-facebooks-face; Chang, 2018.

23 Taylor Hatmaker, Apple Banned Facebook's Onavo App from the App Store for Gathering App Data, *Techcrunch*, 22 August 2018, https://techcrunch. com/2018/08/22/apple-facebook-onavo/ and Josh Constine, Apple Bans Facebook Research App That Pays Users For Data, *Techcrunch*, 30 January 2019, https://techcrunch.com/2019/01/30/apple-bans-facebook-vpn/.

24 On the Six4Three emails, see House of Commons, 2018b, 2019b; Olivia Solon, and Cyrus Farivar, Mark Zuckerberg Leveraged Facebook User Data to Fight Rivals and Help Friends, Leaked Documents Show, *NBC News*, 16 April 2019, www.nbcnews.com/tech/social-media/mark-zuckerberg-leveraged-face book-user-data-fight-rivals-help-friends-n994706; Mark Zuckerberg, 5 December 2018, www.facebook.com/zuck/posts/10105559172610321.

25 Mark Zuckerberg, A Privacy-Focused Vision for Social Networking, 6 March 2019, www.facebook.com/notes/mark-zuckerberg/a-privacy-focused-vision-for-social-networking/10156700570096634/; Ben Thompson, Facebook's Privacy Cake, *Stratechery*, 7 March 2019, https://stratechery.com/2019/facebooks-pri vacy-cake/; John Arlidge, Zuck's Sorry . . . That He Hasn't Got Even More of Your Data, *Sunday Times Business Section*, 10 March 2019, 8; Hannah Murphy, How Facebook Could Target Ads in Age of Encryption, *Financial Times*, 27 March 2019, www.ft.com/content/0181666a-4ad6-11e9-bbc9-6917dce3dc62.

26 On start-ups, see, for example, Noah Kulwin's interview with Roger McNamee, You Have a Persuasion Machine Unlike Anything Created in History, *New York* magazine, April 2018, http://nymag.com/intelligencer/2018/04/roger-mcnamee-early-facebook-investor-interview.html; Claire Ballentine, Google-Facebook Dominance Hurts Ad Tech Firms, Speeding Consolidation, *New York Times*,

12 August 2018, www.nytimes.com/2018/08/12/technology/google-facebook-dominance-hurts-ad-tech-firms-speeding-consolidation.html; Steve Levine, US Start-Ups Are in a Surprising 13-Year Slump, *Axios*, 27 May 2018, www.axios.com/startups-slump-13-years-artificial-intelligence-us-ef914164-78f7-4783-b912-2ea50a06968d.html; James Williams, Facebook's Fundamental Problem? Mark Zuckerberg Can't Innovate, *Wired*, 12 June 2018, www.wired.co.uk/article/alternative-business-models-for-facebook; James Pethokoukis, A New Analysis Takes a Shot at the Idea Big Tech Has Created a 'Kill Zone' for Start-Ups, American Enterprise Institute, 12 July 2018, www.aei.org/publication/a-new-analysis-takes-a-shot-at-the-idea-big-tech-has-created-a-kill-zone-for-startups/.

27 Danny Fortson, Facebook Plot to Launch Own 'Currency', *Sunday Times Business*, 13 May 2018, 3; Emily Glazer, Deepa Seetharaman, AnnaMaria Andriotis, Facebook to Banks: Give Us Your Data, We'll Give You Our Users, *Wall Street Journal*, 6 August 2018, www.wsj.com/articles/facebook-to-banks-give-us-your-data-well-give-you-our-users-1533564049; Steven Levy, Inside Facebook's AI Machine, *Wired*, 23 February 2017, www.wired.com/2017/02/inside-facebooks-ai-machine/; Kurt Wagner, Mark Zuckerberg, in His Own Words, on Why AR Is Facebook's Next Big Platform Bet', *Recode*, 18 April 2017, www.recode.net/2017/4/18/15315764/mark-zuckerberg-facebook-augmented-reality-ar-f8-glasses; Elizabeth Dwoskin and Emily Rahala, Facebook Plans to Open Subsidiary in China After Being Locked Out of the Country for Years, *Washington Post*, 24 July 2018, www.washingtonpost.com/business/economy/facebook-opens-subsidiary-in-china-after-being-locked-out-of-the-country-for-years/2018/07/24/f835dd34-8f5a-11e8-b769-e3fff17f0689_story.html?utm_term=.48cac0d437ab; Dave Lee, Facebook Made China Censorship Tool, *BBC News* online, 23 November 2016, www.bbc.co.uk/news/technology-38073949.

2   Silicon values
Big tech, small state

> We've never seen anything quite like Facebook, where, while we were play-
> ing on our phones and apps, our democratic institutions seem to have been
> upended by frat boy billionaires from Silicon Valley.
> – Canadian MP Charlie Angus, November 2018[1]

On 9 June 1972, the Board of Trustees of Stanford University appointed the
Welsh cultural critic Raymond Williams as a visiting professor of political
science for the winter quarter 1972–3 at a salary of $7,000. During his time
at Stanford, Williams and his wife, Joy, carried out the research which led
to his book *Television: Technology and Cultural Form* (TTCF). In the Raymond Williams archive at Swansea University, you can find notes on new
technological developments in cable and computing, including a television
programme on KQED, the 'community-supported non-commercial public
television station for the San Francisco Bay Area and northern California',
where a teacher walks a Palo Alto school class through a computer lesson
followed by an item with a Stanford professor explaining how computers
can be used to study reading strengths and how one central computer could
support all schools in the area in the future.

Williams, whose work is a resource for contemporary Internet scholars
like Zizi Papacharissi and Thomas Streeter, wrote,

> San Francisco is a beautiful city, probably the most genuinely and
> actively cosmopolitan in the world. In its Bay Area there are two world-
> ranking universities and half a dozen others.

But he noted the contradictions, the imbalance of resources between public
and private institutions and the poverty:

> there, in wealthy California – on its own, the ninth-richest state in the
> world – you only have to travel on public transport to see the real poverty,

not only of so many Blacks and Chicanos and some Chinese, but of poor whites, living hard.[2]

Almost forty years later, Alice Marwick, who spent nine months carrying out ethnographic research in Silicon Valley from 2008–2009, wrote 'Silicon Valley culture depends on undocumented labor to build microchips, clean offices, and mow the lawns of technology workers relocated from Bangalore, Shanghai, Dublin and Des Moines'.

Of 1970s California, Williams notes 'among the jets and the military electronics there is an extraordinary, almost tactile privatisation'. The final injunction he was given is worth stating:

This is the moment to recall what an intelligent Californian said as we were leaving. . . . 'Don't let them californicate the world'.[3]

Although the name Silicon Valley had been coined in 1971, before Williams arrived in the Bay Area, it did not exist in the public imagination. Today, Silicon Valley is both a place, geographically set in the area around San Francisco Bay, although technically, California's hi-tech environment spills out beyond Silicon Valley itself, and a shorthand description for a set of values, ideologies, practices and narratives. Silicon Valley needs to be considered materially and historically.

Silicon Valley developed on the back of prior industrial investment, which was subsequently reinforced by government and university co-operation and support. Its development has significantly accelerated since the 1990s, with the extraordinary expansion and investment of capital underpinning the digital infrastructures of the 'platform economy'.[4]

Arguably, there were two 'inter-related economies' of Silicon Valley, the first being the circuit, computer, computer networking and software companies and other electronics-based industries and the university departments which interact with them, the second being the network of venture capital, legal and other firms that have grown up around them, which together form an interlocking ecosystem. Venture capital firms have played a powerful role in shaping the development of hi-tech companies in Silicon Valley, including their governance structures, their recruitment strategies and their revenue-raising logic of providing free services in return for advertising. Facebook has benefitted at all stages from a particular fraction of Silicon Valley venture capital, colloquially known as the PayPal Mafia, after their online payment system, one of the first IPO successes of the period after the dotcom crash of 2000.[5]

Surveillance capitalism

Professor Shoshana Zuboff sees Facebook as a pivotal player in the development of 'a deeply intentional and highly consequential new logic of accumulation' that she calls 'surveillance capitalism'. She says that each era of capitalism has developed 'a dominant logic of accumulation', based on data, extraction and analysis. Data become 'a new asset class', and these 'surveillance assets' attract investment which can be called 'surveillance capital'. Surveillance capitalism begats a new logic of accumulation, a new form of politics and social relations which imposes a 'privately administered compliance regime'. In this new system, power, as it is so often, is asymmetrically held. The data monopolies like Google and Facebook know more about the data subjects than citizens do about themselves. Facebook, which Zuckerberg said in 2013 was 'producing this living database of all of this content and the stories of people's lives', is one of the largest operators within surveillance capitalism.[6] Surveillance capitalism is already on its way to being a useful heuristic for legislators such as UK Labour Deputy Leader Tom Watson and Canadian MP Bob Zimmer.[7]

Following the dotcom crash of 2000, new enterprises, driven by the desires of their venture capital backers for rapid growth and massive returns, came to adopt advertising as their core business model, harvesting data on their users to provide better and better precision targeting. This predates Google and Facebook, although these two giants are now the dominant recipients of the growth in digital advertising revenue. Joseph Turow points to the importance of an early 1993 article in the advertising weekly *Adweek* by Michael Schrage, as indicating the way in which advertisers and advertising agencies might turn the Internet to their advantage. One of the world's largest advertisers, Proctor and Gamble, became the pioneer of web advertising. Michael Schrage's brother, Elliot, acted as vice-president of global communications and public affairs for Google and then subsequently in the same role for Facebook, working for Sheryl Sandberg in both jobs.[8]

In April 2018, questioned by a United States Senator about how Facebook made money, a bemused Zuckerberg said, 'Senator, we run ads'. Advertising has been central to Facebook's revenues from the beginning. Facebook sought to sell advertising not on the basis of click-through, as was common with other Internet companies, but on the basis of cost-per-thousand views (known as CPM) as with television advertising. Companies also paid on the basis of CPA (cost per acquisition of a new user), for example through sponsored groups, such as Apple's for fans of its products for which the company paid an overall fee plus a $1 acquisition fee for every user who joined. Facebook reached a deal with Microsoft to sell banner advertising through Microsoft's ad sales network, worth $100 million by 2007. The potential of mining the data of Facebook for micro-targeted advertising at specific groups, which became central to the debates on the Trump election of 2016, began quite early on with the targeting of cheerleaders for a Gwen Stefani song in 2005.[9]

The underpinning discursive logic of Silicon Valley is sometimes called 'cyber-libertarianism', or 'the Californian ideology', 'a contradictory mix of technological determinism and libertarian individualism', fusing 'cultural bohemianism' and 'hi-tech' promising 'a digital utopia' in which 'everybody will be both hip and rich'. The role of the Whole Earth Catalog, and its founder, Stewart Brand, in underpinning the countercultural thinking of many Silicon Valley entrepreneurs, including Apple founder Steve Jobs, is often cited in accounts of the making of the Californian ideology.[10]

For Mark Zuckerberg, seeking to manage charges of political bias from Republicans, Silicon Valley itself is 'an extremely left-leaning place'. Some analysis of Silicon Valley politics has been undertaken. A detailed survey of 600 tech entrepreneurs found significant, if not overwhelming, support for Democrats but that they were largely hostile to trade unions and regulation. In terms of registered voters, registered Democrats have been recorded at just below 50% of Silicon Valley residents consistently over the last 20 years, while registered Republicans have dropped from just over 30% in 1998 to below 20% now.[11]

Vanity capitalism

In 1996, a television play by Dennis Potter, *Cold Lazarus*, was broadcast in the UK, in which, in the year 2368, a team of scientists driven on by a media mogul seek to revive the mind of a 20th-century writer who had died in 1994, at the end of Potter's companion-piece, *Karaoke*. Twenty-third-century Britain is run by US corporations, and experience is largely virtual. The writer's head is being held in a cryonics laboratory owned by a pharmaceuticals plutocrat. The plan to broadcast the writer's memories on television, generating substantial incomes for the media company, is ultimately prevented by an activist for a resistance movement opposed to technocratic control of society, who has found that the writer's mind is seeking to communicate his desire to die forever.[12]

Potter's dystopia seemed a trifle fantastic in 1996. But today perhaps the endgame of neoliberalism has been reached with the assertion that death can be prevented and life extended – for those who can afford it. Calico, the California Life Company, a product of Google Ventures, seeks to identify how to prolong life. Other start-ups exist with the same objective with investors including Big Tech billionaires. Silicon Valley's imaginaries extend not only to life-preservation but to sea-steading – floating ocean cities with 'political autonomy', in other words outside the boundaries of normal government.[13] Activities formerly undertaken by nation-states, such as space exploration, are now the purview of a privileged few billionaires, such as Elon Musk or Jeff Bezos – Big Tech, small state. The intellectual leader of the PayPal Mafia, Peter Thiel, interviewed by Carole Cadwalladr for the *Observer* in 2014, confirmed his desire to challenge the boundaries of mortality, adapting the Welsh poet Dylan Thomas by saying, 'we should not go gently into that good night'.[14]

In her powerful, well-researched book, Emily Chang calls the culture of Silicon Valley *Brotopia*, the boys' club of Silicon Valley. Kate Losse called her book on the early years of Facebook *The Boy Kings*. Silicon Valley's Brotopian libertarianism has given us vanity capitalism. This is not a reference to the post-hoodie makeover of Silicon Valley entrepreneurs.[15] Emily Chang identifies the PayPal Mafia as one of the many reasons Silicon Valley came to be run by young white men of affluence. Kate Losse describes an early glimpse of Peter Thiel at a Facebook party. She suggests that venture capitalists tend to have 'a predilection' for younger versions of themselves. The counterculture was a very male-dominated affair – and Chang shows how the philosophy of 'let it all hang out' today resurfaces in the entitlement attitude of some newly wealthy Silicon Valley entrepreneurs. Feminist critiques of Silicon Valley point out that libertarianism is an ideology aimed precisely at privileged young men with no understanding of the ways in which the unpaid labour of women in raising children and holding together families has underpinned their opportunity.[16]

Chang documents the realities for women in Silicon Valley. 1984 was the high point for women graduating in computer science, and the figures fell for the subsequent two and a half decades. In 2017, 36% of jobs in computing-related industries went to women, and the figures were worse for Google and Facebook. She is alert to the elite status of institutions such as Stanford University, 'where the median annual family income of a Stanford student is $167,500 while the national median is one-third that'. She has written about the ways in which women in Silicon Valley are discriminated against, objectified, sometimes humiliated and often patronised, harassed and on occasions assaulted.

Kate Losse, Facebook employee number 51, recounts her memory of a company memo being sent round which said that all women members of staff should come to work on Zuckerberg's birthday wearing T-shirts with his face on the front. She says the – largely male – engineers were valued more than staff in other positions. She said that 'this boys' world' was 'constructed on the reactionary model of an office from the 1950s. The male engineers were the visionaries and the nontechnical staff – often female, sometimes black, 'were assumed to be duller, incapable of quick and intelligent thought'.

In the early days, Zuckerberg and his lieutenants gave themselves a set of ironic titles. Zuckerberg's was Founder, Master and Commander, Enemy of the State. Early Facebook pages were footnoted 'a Mark Zuckerberg production'. This is not however a biography of Zuckerberg. It's important to focus more on key moments in the company's development than on personal psychodrama.

Chang acknowledges that similar books could be written about Silicon Valley attitudes to race and age. In November 2018, a black former Facebook product manager, Mark S. Luckie, went public on issues of discrimination within the company, which he said also had an impact on black and minority ethnic users.[17]

Kate Losse credits Sheryl Sandberg with making an effort to try to turn around the male culture. Facebook's published data, discussed by Sheryl Sandberg in her congressional hearing in September 2018, indicate that Facebook still has some way to go in its diversity policies. Michelle Obama has been one of those who have criticised Sandberg's urging of women to assert themselves in the workplace, set out in her book *Lean-In*, suggesting that this doesn't address structural issues of discrimination: 'It's not always enough to lean in because that shit doesn't work all the time'.[18]

Vanity capitalism embraces all of the counterculture's narcissism and self-indulgence. There is little room for the state and the public sector. This was the age of John Perry Barlow's infamous cyber-libertarian declaration:

> Governments of the Industrial World, you weary giants of flesh and steel, I come from Cyberspace, the new home of Mind. On behalf of the future, I ask you of the past to leave us alone. You are not welcome among us. You have no sovereignty where we gather.[19]

If governments had no sovereignty in cyberspace, within twenty years, 'Big Tech' capitalist conglomerates certainly did. Mark Zuckerberg, in discussing matters with Sheryl Sandberg when he hired her, honed in on her government experience, saying,

> In a lot of ways Facebook is more like a government than a traditional company. We have this large community of people, and more than other technology companies we're really setting policies.

The legal scholar Frank Pasquale has said that 'Big Tech' companies like Facebook are more than market participants; they are market makers. Over time, they seek to displace government roles, replacing 'the logic of territorial with functional sovereignty', meaning people will be subject to corporate, rather than democratic, control. Faced with resistance by law-makers across the globe, Zuckerberg himself has rowed back on what he once said. When *Recode*'s Kara Swisher said to him in June 2018 that 'some people feel you are a nation-state in a lot of ways', Zuckerberg responded, 'We're not. We're a company'. Scrutiny changes discourse.[20]

For Vaidhyanathan, Facebook is 'the paradigmatic distillation of the Silicon Valley ideology'. It is certainly the paradigm of vanity capitalism, exhibited in its monopoly position, its status as a company controlled by its founder, its driving rhetoric of permissionless innovation and the hacker culture and its technocratic approach to solving global problems.

Vanity capitalism privileges monopoly. This is a particular feature of the digital economy today, but increasingly, the establishment of effective monopolies in particular sectors has also become a demand of leading ven-ture capitalists, notably two who sit on Facebook's board, Peter Thiel and Marc Andreessen.[21] Thiel, whom legal scholar Timothy Wu calls not a lib-ertarian but a 'social Darwinist', wrote in 2014,

> Monopolists can afford to think about things other than making money; non-monopolists can't, . . . Only one thing can allow a business to tran-scend the daily brute struggle for survival: monopoly profits.[22]

As founder, Zuckerberg retained strict control over the company through a series of 'voting agreements' outlined in the IPO filing. Facebook went public, but its founder retained control in an arrangement not uncommon in certain classes of tech stocks. Marc Andreessen argued it protects compa-nies from the machinations of hedge funds and short-sellers, saying, 'it is unsafe to go public today without a dual-class share structure'.[23]

Control structures were further amended in 2016 to allow Zuckerberg to retain control even after transferring stock to the philanthropic foundation which he runs with his wife, Priscilla Chan. In a statement at the time, Face-book's General Counsel accepted

> This is not a traditional governance model, but Facebook was not built to be a traditional company. The board believes that a founder-led approach has been and continues to be in the best interests of Facebook, its stockholders, and the community.

In 2017, when Zuckerberg was undertaking a tour of the United States that many people thought presaged a 2020 run for the presidency, it became known that Facebook's statutes had been changed to allow him to retain control even if he were serving in government office.[24]

In his review of Aaron Sorkin's film about Facebook's creation, *The Social Network*, Larry Lessig notes a key omission. In setting up the company, Zuckerberg didn't need *permission* – from anyone. Silicon Valley's discourse of permissionless innovation, coined by Google's chief Internet evangelist Vincent Cerf, has been adopted by right-wing think-tanks as a counter to the 'precautionary principle' underpinning so much of environmental and health policy. Jonathan Taplin traces how avoiding asking permission, on the Ayn Rand basis of 'who will stop me?' has become a doctrine for some in Silicon Valley.[25]

In his open letter in Facebook's SEC filing for its IPO, Zuckerberg said Facebook's approach was 'the Hacker Way' – striving always for continuous improvement 'learning from smaller iterations rather than trying to get everything right all at once'. He reiterated,

> We have a saying: 'Move fast and break things.' The idea is that if you never break anything, you're probably not moving fast enough.

All staff had to go through a 'Bootcamp' where they learned these principles, even if they were not coders. Alex Fattal says that Facebook has tried to keep an association with its early ideological values through what he calls this 'institutionalised nostalgia'.[26]

Losse says Zuckerberg believed that the best engineers would only join a company where engineers were clearly in the ascendancy. To address the rising cost of housing in the Valley, engineers were offered a subsidy – only after protests was this extended to other staff. Vanity capitalism privileges engineers as logical problem-solvers. Zuckerberg frequently frames challenges – countering terrorism, for example – as an engineering challenge to be solved by AI. This, of course, reinforces the mystique and technical superiority of Silicon Valley and its young engineers. Technical language and knowhow has always been used to allow elite dominance of certain new evolving sectors.[27]

'The moment of any new technology', said Raymond Williams, 'is a moment of choice'. This was a warning against the notion of 'technological determinism', which assumes that a new technology emerges simply from experimentation and changes the society into which it has emerged as we adapt to it. This underpins not only Facebook but its founder's philanthropic approach:

> Our mission is to find new ways to leverage technology, community-driven solutions, and collaboration to accelerate progress in Science, Education, and within our Justice & Opportunity work.

Philanthropy, indeed, is the epitome of vanity capitalism.

Technological determinism also underpins Facebook's internet.org partnership and the Free Basics platform:

> Internet.org is a Facebook-led initiative with the goal of bringing internet access and the benefits of connectivity to the portion of the world that doesn't have them. . . . *The more we connect, the better it gets.*

(my italics)

Martin Moore has documented the moves of Big Tech into education and health. The ambitions of vanity capitalism are boundless, though sometimes there is caution in revealing what these companies do. Mark Zuckerberg was asked about Peter Thiel's Palantir, started with funding from the CIA's venture capital fund, when he gave evidence to the Senate: might they be described as Stanford Analytica? Surprisingly, during his evidence, Zuckerberg said, 'I'm not really that familiar with what Palantir does'.

Vanity capitalism was called out by President Obama, somewhat belatedly, towards the end of his term in 2016. 'Government will never run the way Silicon Valley runs', he said at a technology futures conference.[28] Can these Silicon values survive? Interestingly, one Silicon Valley venture capitalist is starting to question the underlying model. His name? Chamath Palihapitiya, former vice-president for growth at Facebook. He says, 'user acquisition and growth has become such an entrenched part of the Silicon Valley zeitgeist'. He says that his Facebook team made user acquisition a science. But now he fears that the venture capital industry is bidding up costs and creating 'a dangerous, high-stakes Ponzi scheme'.

In April 2019, the ride-sharing company Uber filed for its IPO, warning that it might never make a profit.[29] Truly, under Silicon Valley leadership, vanity capitalism is completely californicated.

Notes

1 International Grand Committee, November 2018.
2 Williams, 1989.
3 The Raymond Williams Collection is in the Richard Burton Archive in Swansea University. The sources referred to here are items WWE/2/1/6/1/18/1; WWE/2/1/14/4/1; WWE/2/1/6/1/18/1; and WWE/2.1/6/1/18/3. See also Williams, 1974, 1989; Marwick, 2013.
4 Marwick, 2013; Berlin, 2017: xiii; Adams et al., 2018; Castells and Hall, 1994; Ferrary and Granovetter, 2009; Srnicek, 2017: 5–6.
5 Vaidhyanathan, 2018. On Facebook's IPO and its 'financialization', see Elmer, 2017; on the Paypal Mafia, see Thiel and Masters, 2014; Chang, 2018; on the Paypal IPO's contemporary importance, Jathon Sapsford and Kate Kelly, *Wall Street Journal*, IPO world holds it breath as Paypal comes out to play, 15 February 2002, www.wsj.com/articles/SB1013729731125738400.

6   Zuboff, 2015, 2019: Zuckerberg as quoted in Alexis C. Madrigal, The Education of Mark Zuckerberg, *The Atlantic*, 20 November 2017, www.theatlantic.com/technology/archive/2017/11/the-mark-zuckerberg-theory-of-community/546290/.

7   For 'surveillance capitalism' as heuristic, see Standing Committee on Access to Information, Privacy and Ethics, House of Commons, Canada, Thursday 10 May 2018, www.ourcommons.ca/DocumentViewer/en/42-1/ETHI/meeting-106/evidence and Tom Watson's Speech on Fixing the Distorted Digital Market, *Labour Party*, 6 February 2019, https://labour.org.uk/press/tom-watson-speech-fixing-distorted-digital-market/.

8   Turow, 2012.

9   Zuckerberg was being questioned by Senator Orrin Hatch: see video at www.nbcnews.com/card/we-run-ads-n864606; on Zuckerberg's engagement with the development of advertising, see Zuckerberg, R, 2013; on Zuckerberg's concerns about advertising and user experience, see Kirkpatrick, 2011: 177; Martinez, 2016, 4; on Facebook's early approach to advertising, see Kirkpatrick, 139–40; on Gwen Stefani and the beginning of micro-targeting, Kirkpatrick, 141–3; on the advertising deal with Microsoft, see Kirkpatrick, 178.

10 Winner, 1997; Barbrook and Cameron, 1996; Foer, 2017: 17–20; Kirkpatrick, 2011; Streeter, 1999; Turner, 2006; Taplin, 2017.

11 Dan Bylan, Silicon Valley 'a very left-leaning place', admits Zuckerberg, *Washington Times*, 10 April 2018, www.washingtontimes.com/news/2018/apr/10/zuckerberg-admits-silicon-valley-extremely-left-le/; Broockman et al., 2017; see also Taplin, 2017; Silicon Valley Index, 2018, *Joint Venture Silicon Valley Institute of Regional Studies*, 81, https://jointventure.org/publications/institute-publications/1640-2018-silicon-valley-index.

12 Potter, 1996.

13 The Sea-steading institute has been founded by Peter Thiel and Milton Friedman's grandson, Patri, www.seasteading.org/about/.

14 Carole Cadwalladr, Peter Thiel: 'We Attribute Too Much To Luck. Luck Is an Atheistic Word for God', *Observer*, 21 September 2014, www.theguardian.com/technology/2014/sep/21/peter-thiel-paypal-luck-atheist-god.

15 Stefani Marsh, Meet the Woman Who Tells Silicon Valley's Billionaires How to Dress, *The Times Magazine*, 27 April 2019, www.thetimes.co.uk/article/meet-the-woman-who-tells-silicon-valleys-billionaire-geeks-how-to-dress-dwb087w3k.

16 See Cohen, 2017: 4; Brugger, 2015; 75; Losse, 2012: 20.

17 Sam Levin, Ex-Facebook Manager: Black Staffers Face Discrimination and Exclusion, *Guardian*, 27 November 2018, www.theguardian.com/technology/2018/nov/27/facebook-race-black-employees-discrimination-accusation. Facebook itself has published diversity data, which indicates how poorly it is doing amongst its senior leadership, particularly in recruiting black and Hispanic tech leaders, though it claims that the situation is improving.

18 Losse, 2012: 25, 75, 169; Chang, 2018, 115, 122, 238–240; Ophelia Garcia Lawler, Michelle Obama Is Done with the Gospel of Lean-in, the Cut, *New York* magazine, 2 December 2018, www.thecut.com/2018/12/michelle-obama-lean-in-becoming-book-tour.html; Tracy Chou, Where Are the Numbers? *Medium*, 11 October 2013, https://medium.com/@triketora/where-are-the-numbers-cb997a57252.

19 On John Perry Barlow and libertarianism, see Steven Johnson, The Political Education of Silicon Valley, *Wired*, 24 July 2018, www.wired.com/story/political-education-silicon-valley/; on *WIRED* magazine itself, see David Karpf, 25 Years of WIRED Predictions: Why the Future Never Arrives, *Wired*, 18 September 2018, www.wired.com/story/wired25-david-karpf-issues-tech-predictions/.

20 Pasquale, 2017; Kirkpatrick, 2011: 254; Kara Swisher, Interview with Mark Zuckerberg, *Recode*, 18 July 2018, www.recode.net/2018/7/18/17575158/mark-zuckerberg-facebook-interview-full-transcript-kara-swisher.

21 Vaidhyanathan, 2018; Foer, 2018; Pasquale, 2018; Davies, 2018.

22 Turow, 2012; Michael Schrage profile, https://executive.mit.edu/faculty/profile/77-michael-schrage, and on Elliott Schrage, see John Battelle, Dinner with Elliott Schrage, 20 April 2006, https://battellemedia.com/archives/2006/04/dinner_with_elliot_schrage and Elliott Schrage's *Facebook* post, 14 June 2018, www.facebook.com/elliot/posts/10155368278417536; Vaidhyanathan, 2018b; Zuboff, 2015, 2019; Peter Thiel, www.wsj.com/articles/peter-thiel-competition-is-for-losers-1410535536.

23 Quoted in Joann S. Lublin and Spencer E. Ante, A Fight in Silicon Valley: Founders Push for Control, *Wall St Journal*, 11 July 2012, www.wsj.com/articles/SB10001424052702303292204577519134168240996.

24 Colin Stretch, Preserving Founder-Led Structure to Focus on the Long Term, 27 April 2016, https://newsroom.fb.com/news/2016/04/q1-earnings-note/; a good discussion of the 'presidential' tour is given in Max Read, Does even Mark Zuckerberg know what Facebook Is? *New York* magazine, 1 October 2017, http://nymag.com/intelligencer/2017/10/does-even-mark-zuckerberg-know-what-facebook-is.html; Danny Fortson, President Zuck, *Sunday Times*, 5 February 2017, www.thetimes.co.uk/article/president-zuck-xdc32xqkv; Hayley Tsukayama, Facebook Shareholders Are Not Happy with How It's Handling Fake News, *Washington Post*, 1 June 2017. Oliver Shah, Investors, Including Legal and General, Demand End to Tech Titans' Control of Shares, *Sunday Times*, 25 November 2018, www.thetimes.co.uk/article/investors-including-legal-general-demand-end-to-tech-titans-control-of-shares-973mn6w3m.

25 Lawrence Lessig, Sorkin vs Zuckerberg, *New Republic*, 1 October 2010, https://newrepublic.com/article/78081/sorkin-zuckerberg-the-social-network; on permissionless innovation: Cerf, 2012; Golumbia, 2014; Dotson, 2015; Thierer, 2016; on Ayn Rand's influence, see Taplin, 2017; Nick Bilton, Silicon Valley's Most Disturbing Obsession, 5 October 2016, www.vanityfair.com/news/2016/10/silicon-valley-ayn-rand-obsession and Jonathan Freedland, The New Age of Ayn Rand: How She Won Over Trump and Silicon Valley, 10 April 2017, www.theguardian.com/books/2017/apr/10/new-age-ayn-rand-conquered-trump-white-house-silicon-valley.

26 See Taplin, 2017. The Zuckerberg letter can be read in full in the archived version of the Facebook IPO filing, www.sec.gov/Archives/edgar/data/1326801/000119312512034517/d287954ds1.htm#toc287954_10. Bucher, 2018: 70; Andrew Bosworth (Boz), Facebook Engineering Bootcamp, 20 November 2009, www.facebook.com/notes/facebook-engineering/facebook-engineering-boot camp/177577963919; Ben Hamilton, Bootcamp Growing Culture at Facebook, 19 January 2010, www.facebook.com/notes/facebook-engineering/bootcamp-growing-culture-at-facebook/249415563919. Fattal, 2012.

27 Marvin, 1988.

28 Moore, 2018. On Palantir, Quentin Hardy, Unlocking Secrets, If Not Its Own Value, *New York Times*, 31 May 2014, www.nytimes.com/2014/06/01/business/unlocking-secrets-if-not-its-own-value.html; Washington Post, 2018a; White House, 2016.

29 Chamath Palihapitiya, Social Capital, Annual Letter to Investors, 2018, https://s3-us-west-2.amazonaws.com/socialcapital-annual-letters/Social+Capital+Inte rim+Annual+Letter,+2018.pdf; Joshua Franklin, Uber Unveils IPO with Warning It May Never Make a Profit, *Reuters*, 11 April 2019, www.reuters.com/article/us-uber-ipo/uber-unveils-ipo-with-warning-it-may-never-make-a-profit-idUSKCN1RN2SK.

3 The benefits of Facebook

> To flatter and follow others, without being flattered and followed in turn, is
> but a state of half enjoyment.
>
> – Jane Austen, *Persuasion*

In April 2018, after Cambridge Analytica captured global attention, Facebook embarked on its biggest-ever advertising campaign to try to rebuild trust. At the heart of the campaign was a television advertisement with a voiced narration (using different actors for different territories) over a collage of images and videos saying,

> We came here for the friends, we got to know the friends of our friends – then our old friends from middle school, our mom (mum in UK and Australian versions), our ex, and our boss (workmates in some versions) joined forces to wish us a happy birthday.
>
> Then we discovered our uncle used to play in a band, and realized he was young once, too. And we found others just like us and, just like that, felt a little less alone.
>
> But then something happened. We had to deal with spam, clickbait, fake news, and data misuse. That's going to change.

The slot ended with the words 'Here Together'. Television advertising was accompanied by cinema, radio, social media slots, print and billboards. Some advertising emphasised 'Fake News is not our friend' ('Fake news is not your friend' in some versions), 'Fake accounts are not our friends' or 'Data misuse is not our friend'. The TV ad was soon characterised as being part of Facebook's 'apology tour' and rapidly sparked parodies.[1]

It wasn't the first Facebook advertising campaign following the events of 2016. Full-page advertisements ran in major US newspapers as Facebook headed for congressional hearings on Russian meddling in the autumn of 2017. The weekend that the *Observer*, the *New York Times* and *Channel Four* broke the Cambridge Analytica story, Facebook ran full-page ads in major broadsheets in the US and the UK, saying, 'We have a responsibility to protect your information. If we can't, we don't deserve it', over Mark Zuckerberg's signature. Facebook continued to run print advertising during 2018, alerting readers to what it was doing to combat bullying online, directing parents to online guides for how their children could stay safe online, pointing users to online information on what Facebook did with their personal information and how they could control that and informing them of the steps that Facebook had taken to keep people safe online by recruiting more 'safety experts' under the slogan 'what matters to you, matters to us'.

Prior to Cambridge Analytica, Facebook had also run a series of ads in early 2018 illustrating how small businesses in the UK had benefitted from their association with Facebook. With the strapline 'Let's get to work' the advertisements focused on case studies of small businesses who had advertised on Facebook:

> James sells British Ale to customers across Italy, America and Japan.
> Charlotte's queue gets longer and longer and longer.
> Jacqui works out of her flat in Hackney and has a shop in Seoul.
> Guy started with one box of vegetables. Now we help him sell two million across the UK.
> Last year, Mark averaged a new customer every day.
> Holly, Paul and team meet customers from Brick Lane to Bahrain.

The companies featured included real-ale producers, butchers, craft makers, organic farmers and hairdressers.[2] I recognised the company in one of the advertisements: 'David and Clare ship jeans around the world and create jobs in their town' – the inspiring story of Hiut Denim. As its website says,

> Cardigan is a small town of 4,000 good people. 400 of them used to make jeans. They made 35,000 pairs a week. For three decades.
>
> Then one day the factory closed. It left town. But all that skill and knowhow remained. Without any way of showing the world what they could do.
>
> That's why we have started The Hiut Denim Company. To bring manufacturing back home. To use all that skill on our doorstep. And to breathe new life into our town.

David and Claire Hieatt, who previously owned the clothing firm Howie's, sold to Timberland in 2007 but bought back by its management in 2012, set up their business in 2012 to create high-quality denim jeans using the skills of former factory workers. The company now has customers around the world. David, who had a background in advertising, told the BBC in 2017,

> 'The interesting thing about social media for me is that up until Facebook, Instagram, Twitter and SnapChat you had to have a huge budget in order to tell your story,' he says.

Hiut Denim has also created the 'Do Lectures', an annual event in West Wales, with associated workshops and talks, with their emphasis on encouraging people to take a first step to change things for the better, learning from the successes of others. In 2018, the company achieved greater global attention when the actress Meghan Markle wore a pair of their jeans on a visit to Cardiff.[3]

I spoke to David about the company's engagement with Facebook. Initially, they had not used the platform, but then they attended an Instagram-led meeting in London where they learned about its power to build community and help sell their jeans. They began most heavily on Instagram but now marketed through Facebook as well. They have used their Facebook page for organic connection with their audience but also used Facebook's advertising tools, such as the Lookalike Audience tool. David's verdict was that the experience had definitely worked 'from the small maker's perspective, it allowed them to find an audience they would have otherwise had to spend more serious money to reach'. They could not afford TV or press advertising – even local press. They used other communications routes – such as their newsletter, which was one of their primary tools but also workshops and earned publicity – they had recently been featured in the *Wall Street Journal* at the time I interviewed him.[4] They were invited onto the Facebook small business council, which gave them insights on how to grow, master classes and networking with other makers, which enabled them to learn from the experience of others in the UK and indeed in the United States. Their business was featured in Facebook press advertising in the UK and poster advertising in London, which helped to build awareness. Facebook was second in importance to their newsletter for their marketing. Without it, they would not have been so successful.

Hiut Denim also featured in a television advertisement under the same 'Let's get to work' strapline, as did another company based in Wales, Recycle Scooters. This is a business run from Cwmbach at the top of the Cynon Valley by Helen Walbey and her husband, Stephen. Helen explained to me,

> I was approached to be one of the six businesses in the campaign. . . .
> I had an entire day filming with a professional film crew, and a number
> of Facebook team members, to put together this national advertising

campaign. They included twenty businesses when they were filming, and six of us made the cut. I was one of the featured businesses.

At the time I interviewed Helen, she was a post-graduate student in Cardiff Business School, where I work, but she was leaving for a job overseas as the Global Head for Women's Financial Inclusion and Gender at an organisation called the Alliance for Financial Inclusion, which in ten years has brought about 630 million people access to banking.[5] She told me, 'we were trading for fourteen years and we had a Facebook Page pretty much from when we started, and we sold globally, through eBay predominantly'. Facebook was used to promote the business. On their Facebook page,[6] which has over 4,700 likes and followers, they would share information and news about the motorcycle industry, new regulations and so on. They would undertake a small amount of advertising on Facebook as well to direct people to promotions on their eBay shop.

> We would sometimes do just three days, or we would do a longer promotion over perhaps a fortnight, but we used all the data we were getting back to identify when the best times were to put sales on, the type of people who engaged.

She said, 'the Facebook analytics are very good if you know how to use them to enable you to target very specific people with very targeted promotions and advertising'. Demographic information – for example, the age range of those clicking through, was particularly valuable. Facebook also increased 'the local footfall' to their industrial unit. Helen invested time in learning about how better to market:

> So there's something called Facebook Blueprint,[7] and Facebook Blueprint is their database of tutorials and workshops. . . . I went through ever such a lot of the Blueprint stuff and learnt how to actually drive Facebook. If you really do start running these micro-campaigns and then tweaking one of the metrics on it and then checking what kind of response you're getting, you can really target things very well. And it does. . . . It does work. But it only works because they have such a vast amount of data on us all.

Helen was actively involved as the Federation of Small Business's (FSB) National Policy Portfolio Chair for Diversity and Inclusion. When Facebook ran their #SheMeansBusiness campaign to promote women entrepreneurs, they chose a number of small businesses run by women:

Because there are no scrapyards that are run by women, I happened to be one of the businesses that they chose. Because also, if you think about the visuals of Facebook, my business is perfect for that kind of visual, because it's all brightly coloured things, it's lots of dirty things, it's lots of noisy things, it's lots of things that can explode. For video footage it looks great. And of course the fact that I'm little and female doing something in such a stereotypical male industry worked very well for what they were trying to achieve.

Helen was invited to speak at the launch of #Shemeansbusiness. She was invited to Facebook's European small business summit, called GATHER, in Brussels in 2018, and also to the following year's in Dublin. 'Incredibly slick, very very very multi-national . . . they had entrepreneurs from all across Europe'. The events focused on Facebook, 'Instagram, AI, machine learning, lots of stuff with using metrics again'. Facebook's Europe, Middle East, Africa senior management team were present, and Sheryl Sandberg flew in to give keynotes.

Helen subsequently became uncomfortable about Facebook's data challenges and deactivated her personal Facebook account.

Academics call the technical opportunities offered by social media companies 'affordances': they provide real benefits for the user, conditioned by the design features which the technologies present.[8] The affordances offered by Facebook, Instagram and WhatsApp are real and utilised and experienced daily by users on a personal, civic or commercial basis. Experiences like those of Hiut Denim and Recycle Scooters provide examples of why, despite the #deletefacebook campaigns and the departure of some high-profile celebrities, Facebook is here to stay. Facebook has given brand projection to many small businesses on an affordable basis. Facebook executives, particularly Sheryl Sandberg, like to cite examples of small businesses amongst the seven million advertisers which have benefitted from a Facebook presence.[9] The solution to the challenges that Facebook raises is not to delete it but to regulate it.

Given the high percentage of people who now use or have used Facebook around the world, there is little need today to explain the process of setting up an account; creating a profile; uploading photographs, videos and news items; adding friends; joining groups or creating Groups or Pages; exchanging messages; organising events; receiving notifications; liking; commenting; and sharing. As Zeynep Tufekci says,

Facebook has been adopted rapidly in almost every country where it has been introduced because it fulfills a basic human desire: to connect with family and friends.

Over $1 billion has been raised for charities on Facebook. New affordances are created without users asking for them – Marketplace allowing people to list things for sale or to find things to purchase, for example. Some – e.g., Facebook Stories – ape those of other platforms, like Snap-Chat. Facebook's affordances are felt and utilised on a familial, professional, communal, societal and national basis, although some recent UK research has suggested that people may be moving away from Facebook as their primary means of keeping in contact with friends, while gravitating to other Facebook-owned services like WhatsApp. This was particularly true of younger people. These usage patterns have been reported in the US as well.[10]

Facebook's ownership of Instagram, WhatsApp and Messenger has expanded the range of affordances. They are amongst the top 5 downloaded applications on the two major mobile phone application stores, Apple and Google Play. Over 50% of Americans surveyed in April 2018 did not know that Facebook owned Instagram.[11] Social media platforms, notes Zizi Papacharissi, can amplify the tendency to articulate lifestyle values, but these themselves can become political statements. Instagram, having started as a pure photographic site with cool filters has become something of a platform for design, food and lifestyle photography, where ordinary users follow celebrities and influencers: photography, as Siva Vaidhyanathan says, following Susan Sontag, is addictive. Zeynep Tufekci notes that WhatsApp as an encrypted messaging service offers specific affordances, not least to social movement activists. Messenger as an app is an expansion of the chat and messaging sections of the original desktop Facebook application, which is itself becoming heavily commercialised with consumer advertising, business accounts, gaming and other services.[12]

Like Facebook, Instagram has added features over time, such as video, Stories and now Instagram TV. Instagram has become more commercialised over time with advertising or sponsored posts now featuring in users' feeds more regularly and an interactive 'Instagram Shopping' feature, which has developed the platform into an e-commerce site, and the international media is full of stories about people claiming to be 'Instagram influencers', including parents who are marketing their children, some of them very young indeed. These 'influencers' – essentially celebrities or people with large numbers of followers, are paid to endorse products and services in their social media posts. This practice is now being regulated by the FTC in the US. WhatsApp and Facebook Messenger are also increasingly commercialised spaces, with advertising on Messenger being rolled out in 2018.[13]

Histories of the early days of Facebook are littered with references to the engineers communicating on AOL Instant Messenger, and Facebook's former vice-president of growth had been its vice-president. It is no surprise then that messaging plays such a significant role in Facebook's new growth strategy. The affordances of WhatsApp at first glance appear more like text messaging, with the advantages that messages sent over Wi-Fi are free and wholly encrypted via end-to-end encryption. The ease of forming groups and circulating material within them is another affordance which is obvious. Users can also send 'broadcast messages' to all who have their mobile phone number. Chats are stored in a user-friendly way, and WhatsApp messages can now be used on desktop computers as well. They are used by protest movements, political parties and civic movements.[14]

Facebook Messenger is more closely integrated with a user's Facebook profile than WhatsApp. Facebook Messenger does not use end-to-end encryption but encrypts messages by default from the sender to its server and then encrypts them again between the server and the recipient. Unlike WhatsApp, there is no limit to the number of photographs that can be sent. However, unlike WhatsApp, deletion of messages is not at present possible, though a deletion feature has been promised ever since it was revealed that Mark Zuckerberg was able to delete his messages.[15] In December 2017, Facebook launched Messenger Kids for under-13s, aimed at an audience without phones, where parental approval is required for affiliation, there are no ads and data is not collected.

Less than twenty-five miles north of Cardiff Business School, where this book was largely scoped and written, lies the village of Blaencwm, nestling in the hills of the valley known as the Rhondda Fawr, not far from the flat-topped mountain of Pen Pych, styled by the UK's Ordnance Survey mapping service as the Rhondda Valley's own Table Mountain.[16] In minutes, you can walk from Blaencwm to the location of a disused two-mile railway tunnel opened in 1890, which used to transport coal from the former coal-mining Rhondda Valleys to the ports of Port Talbot, Baglan, Neath and Swansea for shipping all over the world but closed 50 years ago. In recent years, there has been a growing civic society campaign to have the Rhondda and Swansea Bay Railway Tunnel, to give its full title, re-opened as the longest tunnel for cycling and walking in Europe.

The Rhondda Tunnel Society, formed in 2014 with the simple objective of siting the recently discovered cornerstone for the tunnel in a suitable location, has grown, as its website says, 'with the aid of modern social media', into a campaign to have the Tunnel re-opened, with a supportive worldwide membership. As the local constituency Assembly member, I helped the society to get initial funding for a scoping study to assess the feasibility of its re-opening. The society maintains a Facebook group with over 4,000 members, which has grown steadily since Welsh media reporting on the society's plans in early 2015 and has a Facebook page with 1,700 likes. Facebook has been a platform for the society in communicating with its members locally and around the world; sharing information on media coverage and support from the Welsh government and local government, celebrities and politicians; welcoming new members by name; and fundraising. What began as a romantic vision in the mind of its founder, Stephen Mackey, has developed, through the energies of the society's committee and the organisational affordances of social media like Facebook, into a well-supported campaign with institutional backing, engineering expertise and extensive coverage in popular mainstream print, radio and television media.

The Rhondda Tunnel Society is just one example of a strong network of civic organisations in the Rhondda Valleys which actively use Facebook to communicate between members, organise, arrange events, campaign and share information across the two valleys and within their villages and towns.[17] Facebook is used as a communications medium between citizens and their elected representatives at local council, National Assembly for Wales and UK Parliament levels. Information, local news, photographs and history are shared, friendships and family relationships sustained and life events recorded, celebrated, mourned, remembered or discussed. Facebook has been a platform for campaigns over local educational and health issues, such as school and hospital re-organisation. My own Facebook activity was like that of many other politicians, judging from academic research.[18]

In Wales, the English and Welsh languages have equal legal status. Annual survey results suggest 29% of people over three can speak Welsh from a population of roughly 3 million. From 2008 onwards, Facebook made it possible to translate the Facebook interface into languages other than English, beginning with languages which made the most compelling financial case.[19] Facebook's interface has been translated into Welsh by a willing group of volunteers, some of whom responded to an advertisement and others who saw friends discussing the translation project on Facebook, giving Welsh-speaking users the infrastructure of a mass platform to conduct conversations through their preferred language. Robert Jones, one of those taking part in the translation exercise, told me,

> the translation interface was easy to use, and the instructions were easy to understand. The process was simple.

He recalled debate involving people from different backgrounds on the nature of language to be used – informal or formal, northern dialect or southern – not just scholars or linguists. He emphasised the importance of having the interface in Welsh:

> As a someone who lives and comes from abroad, who works professionally and personally in different languages, having an interface in

Welsh is very important to me. It gives me another chance to see and interact with the language every day.[20]

Some of those involved in the translation project, like Chris Griffiths, one of the most prolific translators of web applications, had taken part in translating applications before. He was often one of the highest-ranked translators of Facebook into Welsh. Chris said he got angry when companies failed to provide digital services in Welsh. He loved the idea of crowd-sourcing translations, which was a great way to involve people in achieving the goal of a Welsh language service. He noted that Facebook wanted its service to be available in all languages but recognised this was probably for reasons different to those undertaking the translations. The important thing from his point of view was that the service was available to him and others to use in Welsh, and it meant that Welsh-speakers less comfortable in the English language, including older people, could use it in their own language. It also meant that Welsh-learners could switch their interface to Welsh, which might help them in their learning experience. Another of those involved, Sion Jobbins, said he felt Facebook could have provided a Welsh-language interface themselves, as they had the money and it would fit their objectives of rolling out the platform globally. Having the interface in Welsh benefitted Facebook's objective of being a 'social' network. It raised the profile of Welsh, which was very important, and it made sense for a company that talks about 'society' and 'connecting people' to do so in the different languages of different people and communities in the world. The existence of a Welsh interface was positive for the Welsh language. It also helped to ensure that people who do not normally see Welsh content or type and read Welsh do so. Without it, he said, there was 'a very real risk, and it is real, that English is the 'normal' and default Facebook language and that Welsh speakers connect to each other, or to a larger audience, only in English'.[21]

Facebook is used in campaigns across the world. An early example is given in Clay Shirky's 'techno-optimist' *Here Comes Everybody*, where he explains how students in the UK responded to the HSBC bank's decision to start charging graduates, originally recruited as students with promises of interest-free overdrafts, for any overdrafts they ran in 2007. A campaign coordinated by Cambridge Student Union Vice-President Wes Streeting forced HSBC to drop its policy: central to the campaign was the Facebook Group 'Stop the Great HSBC Graduate Rip-off'. Wes is now a Labour MP in the UK House of Commons. He told me,

When HSBC announced their change in policy to charge graduates for their overdraft facilities, universities had broken up for the summer and so our traditional methods of mobilising students on campuses weren't available. We needed to act fast as we knew this would be a dangerous precedent. I set up a Facebook group – almost like a petition really – and it fast became a place where students and graduates started sharing information about switching bank accounts and organising protests. After we won our campaign, HSBC told me that they were tracking Facebook activity and the high correlation it had with students and graduates switching accounts, which is one of the reasons the bank backed down.

In the last year, Mark Zuckerberg has spoken more about the importance of Facebook Groups, revealing that 1.4 billion people use Facebook Groups every month, and 200 million of the Facebook Groups are deemed meaningful. For many people, 'they become the most important part of your Facebook experience and a big part of your real-world social infrastructure'.[22] What goes on in Groups is largely private to the Groups, which are policed by the Group administrators.

It's clear that Mark Zuckerberg wants those Facebook affordances to be widely understood, giving examples in his written evidence to Congress in April 2018 of its role in the #MeToo movement and the March for Our Lives and fundraising after Hurricane Harvey. Facebook's engagement in disaster relief commenced on an industrial scale with a call from the White House to assist after the Haitian earthquake in January 2010.[23]

Accounts of Facebook's early days often cite the example of the anti-FARC movement in Colombia, which was sustained by a Facebook page set up in 2008 by the unemployed engineer Oscar Morales, with 350,000 supporters. Facebook is often cited as a platform for protest, perhaps reaching its zenith in this context during the Arab Spring, when, like other communications media before it, it was actively promoted as a causal trigger of the growing range of protests which took place. The geo-political context reflected themes enunciated by US Secretary of State Hillary Clinton on Internet freedom a year or so before.[24]

The journalist Hannes Grassegger has written, 'The Arab spring was the best marketing for Facebook ever'. In the case of Egypt, it was perhaps the CNN interview with one of the organisers of protests in Cairo's Tahrir Square, the Google engineer Wael Ghonim, on the day that Egypt's President Mubarak announced he would step down in February 2011, which promoted the idea that Facebook was responsible for driving forward revolution. Asked by the CNN anchor, what was next after Tunisia and Egypt, Ghonim replied, 'Ask Facebook'. The CNN presenter suggested he was giving Facebook a lot of credit for the uprising. Ghonim replied,

> Yes, for sure. I want to meet Mark Zuckerberg one day, and thank him, actually. . . . This revolution started online, this revolution started on Facebook.

The Egyptian revolution, along with other movements such as Occupy, has resulted in a considerable amount of scholarship on Facebook.[25]

Ghonim recalls, 'We would post a video on Facebook that would be shared by 50,000 people, on their walls, within a few hours'. He was referring to the Facebook pages *We are all Khaled Said* (in English) and *@ elshaheeed* (in Arabic), which are still accessible on Facebook. The growth in support for these pages showed how the revolt against Mubarak spread throughout a widening spectrum of Egyptian society. Activists subsequently stressed that organisation on the ground was key and social media platforms simply tools.[26]

Khaled Said was a young businessman from Alexandria tortured to death in June 2010 by Egyptian policemen, whose murder was not properly investigated by the Egyptian authorities even after interventions by European Union representatives. The pages became the focus for organising and posting material about the protests in Egypt. Facebook had been available in Arabic from 2009. It had 4 million users in Egypt by late 2010. Ghonim posted a Facebook invitation to a rally in Tahrir Square on 25 January 2011. That was widely shared on Facebook and thousands turned up. Facebook, however, deactivated the 'We are all Khaled Said' page in November 2010 because it violated their policy that pages and profiles must be attributable to people's real names. After international protests, which resulted in an Egyptian woman living abroad agreeing to give her name to the page, it was reinstated.[27]

Social media like Facebook, says Zizi Papacharissi, invite people to 'feel their own place' in relation to developing current events, enabling them to make sense and meaning of them through their emotional reactions captured within the story-telling infrastructure of these media. The technologies provide the network, but the narratives connect us. They make visible what Raymond Williams referred to as 'structures of feeling', the mood and feel of a particular historical moment existing before movements can begin to articulate a narrative.[28]

Egypt is probably the best-known example of Facebook's role in protest, though it features in a wide range of protest movements, from Iranian women protesting the veil and Indian women surreptitiously using Facebook for communication beyond the home to the Occupy movement and protests against Erdogan's Turkish government. As Zeynep Tufekci remarks, in her rich and important book on social media and political protest,

> Thanks to a Facebook page, perhaps for the first time in history, an internet user could click yes on an electronic invitation to a revolution. Hundreds of thousands did so, in full view of their online networks of strong and weak ties, all at once.

Facebook helps protest movements develop their 'narrative capacity', their ability to frame issues in ways that appeal to supporters, allowing them to organise, to raise funds and to generate mainstream media coverage. She calls it the 'indispensable platform', providing a variety of organisational and communications needs for social movements. The optimism of the Arab Spring did not last. Ghonim himself is more critical now. Facebook, like other communications technologies before it, was a facilitator of protest, but what ultimately matters is year-by-year on-the-ground mobilisation.[29]

From small business marketing to political protest, the maintenance of personal networks of friends, family, colleagues and acquaintances with stronger or weaker ties, for alerting friends and family about one's safety during disasters or terrorist incidents through Facebook Safety Check, for civic and political organisation more generally and for viral charity fund-raisers like 2014's the Ice-Bucket Challenge in which 17 million videos, viewed 10 billion times by 440 million people, were uploaded to Facebook, Facebook's features are widely used.[30]

Those who've worked at Facebook are conscious of the changes that they have wrought. Their impressions dovetail with what academic research on uses and gratifications records on our need for self-affirmation, on social media use as acts of performance, as bonding or competitive activities, as helping us maintain wide networks of both strong and weak ties. The affordances of Facebook are real and have been given due attention by academic researchers over time. Facebook, says Roberto Simanowski, 'is cool and it's fun'; it gives people 'the exciting feeling of being a public person with a history, a series of photographs, an audience, and fan letters'. It is a space where people can narrate their lives 'as an adventure'. Facebook's popularity demonstrates that we are social beings, and it meets our need for connection. It allows us to express ourselves, principally to our friends and family, gaining their approbation for the self that we publicly present. It is, generally speaking, our friends and family who remain the key audience for users of Facebook. Facebook has become a convenient way in which people access both reported and sometimes first-hand participant news – and it has provided a not uncontroversial platform for media organisations themselves.[31]

Although early on researchers reported concerns that Facebook users tended to be white, affluent and middle class, more recent developments have shown its growing importance across all demographics, including under-represented groups. As the #deletefacebook movement got underway in 2018, some pointed out the serious difficulties of isolation that might happen to the housebound.[32]

Increasingly, economists are looking at whether it is possible to estimate the value of Facebook to the economy overall and to individual users. The debate on these calculations is controversial. As we shall see in the next chapter, Facebook may be a valuable service, but users pay for it with their attention – and their data.[33]

Notes

1 Jeff Beer, Facebook Says Sorry (sort of) in Its Biggest Ever Ad Campaign, *Fast Company*, 25 April 2018, www.fastcompany.com/40563382/facebook-says-sorry-sort-of-in-its-biggest-ever-ad-campaign; I-Helen Sherwood, 'Facebook's Apology Tour Continues in Nationwide Ad Campaign, *Adage*, 25 April, 2018; John Oliver, John Oliver – Last Week Tonight – New Facebook Ad Campaign, www.youtube.com/watch?time_continue=40&v=8ROdly-iIYQ; Zeynep Tufekci, 2018, op. cit. Emma Stafansky, Mark Zuckerberg Escalates Apology Tour with Full-Page Ad, *Vanity Fair*, 25 March 2018, www.vanityfair.com/news/2018/03/mark-zuckerberg-escalates-facebook-cambridge-analytica-apology-tour-with-full-page-ad: Issie Lapowsky, The Biggest Political Advertiser on Facebook Is . . . Facebook, *Wired*, 23 October 2018, www.wired.com/story/top-political-advertiser-on-facebook-is-facebook/ and for examples see the Facebook Ad Archive, www.facebook.com/ads/archive/?active_status=all&ad_type=all&country=US&view_all_page_id=20531316728.
2 For a more wary take on the benefit of Facebook advertising to entrepreneurs, see Richard Reed, There Is Only One Winner When Start-Ups Advertise on Facebook, *Sunday Times Business*, 3 September 2017, 10.
3 Will Smale and Greg Brosnan, How a Welsh Jeans Firm Became a Cult Global Brand, *BBC News* Online, 13 December 2017, www.bbc.co.uk/news/business-42237426; www.hiutdenim.co.uk; www.thedolectures.com; Amanda Powell, How the 'Meghan Markle' Jeans Company Founders Hope to Inspire You with Videos and a New Book, *Western Mail*, 15 October 2018, www.walesonline.co.uk/business/how-meghan-markle-jeans-company-15266228.
4 I interviewed David by telephone on 30 January 2019.
5 See Alliance for Financial Inclusion, www.afi-global.org.I interviewed Helen in Cardiff Business School on 12 March 2019.
6 Recycle Scooters, www.facebook.com/RecycleScootersandBikes/.
7 Facebook Blueprint Helps Businesses Market Across the Facebook Platforms, www.facebook.com/business/ads/ad-formats?ref=ens_rdr; on FTC rules on Instagram influencer marketing, see Paris Martineau, Inside the Pricey War to Influence Your Instagram Feed, *Wired*, 18 November 2018, www.wired.com/story/pricey-war-influence-your-instagram-feed/.
8 I use 'affordances' in a broad sense in this chapter.
9 See for example, Sheryl Sandberg's introductory comments in Facebook's Fourth Quarter and Full Year Results Conference Call, 30 January 2019, https://s21.q4cdn.com/399680738/files/doc_financials/2018/Q4/Q4-2018-earnings-call-transcript.pdf.
10 People raise over $1 billion for the causes they care about on Facebook, 14 November 2018 https://newsroom.fb.com/news/2018/11/people-raise-over-1-billion/; Tufekci, 2017: 29.
11 A majority of Americans don't know that Facebook owns Instagram, Duck-DuckGo, 9 April 2018, https://spreadprivacy.com/facebook-instagram/.
12 Katrina Burroughs, How Does Your Space Square Up? *Sunday Times Home* section, 23 September 2018, 12–13; Oliver Wainwright, Picture This, *Guardian*

Review, 24 November 2018, 32–33; Vaidhyanathan, 2018: 48–49; Tufekci, 2017; Nieborg and Helmond, 2019; Papacharissi, 2015: 7.

13 www.facebook.com/business/instagram/shopping; Harry Shukman, Toddler Ralphie Bags £10,000 as Instagram Influencer, *The Times*, 3 December 2018, www.thetimes.co.uk/article/toddler-ralphie-earns-10-000-as-instagram-influ encer-gsj29xhr9?shareToken=a561cf871d85f9ce663b738d63d29845; on adver-tising on Messenger, see Facebook Fourth Quarter earnings call, note 8 above; Tanvi Dubey, This Woman Entrepreneur Is Earning Millions Selling Sarees via WhatsApp, *Your Story*, 15 November 2018, https://yourstory.com/2018/11/ woman-entrepreneur-selling-sarees-whatsapp.

14 WhatsApp groups are regularly mentioned in discussions of parliamentary mobilisation, for example, see Lucy Fisher, Corbyn Marshalls Support via WhatsApp, *The Times*, 5 June 2018, www.thetimes.co.uk/article/corbyn-mar shals-support-via-whatsapp-2j8qh95w2?shareToken=edc83e0eb975787efa14c 04521f060dd; Tim Shipman, Brexit: The Week When It All Fell Apart, *Sunday Times*, 24 March 2019, www.thetimes.co.uk/article/brexit-the-week-when-it-all-fell-apart-5635k7mz0. Losse, 2012: 11, 60.

15 WhatsApp vs Facebook Messenger: 5 Main Differences Users Should Know, *Business Today*, 7 January 2019, www.businesstoday.in/buzztop/buzztop-fea ture/whatsapp-vs-facebook-messenger-5-main-differences-users-should-know/ story/306784.html; Matt Novak, Remember When Facebook Promised a Delete Button for Your Sent Messages? *Gizmodo*, 10 October 2018, https://gizmodo.com/ remember-when-facebook-promised-a-delete-button-for-you-1829655473.

16 Tracy Purnell, Circular Walk Around Pen Pych Mountain, *Ordnance Survey*, https://getoutside.ordnancesurvey.co.uk/adventures/pen-pych-mountain/; www.rhonddatunnelsociety.co.uk; David Owens, How the World Fell in Love with the Rhondda Tunnel Again and Again in 2015, *WalesOnline*, 23 Decem-ber 2015, www.walesonline.co.uk/news/wales-news/how-world-fell-love-rhondda-10640382; www.facebook.com/groups/rhonddatunnelsociety/; www. facebook.com/RhonddaTunnelSociety/; Thomas Deacon, Breakthrough for Rhondda Tunnel Society Yields Rare Finds, *Western Mail*, 7 May 2018, 23; Steven Morris, Welsh Rail Tunnel Could Re-Open as Two-Mile Walk and Cycle Route, *Guardian*, 12 August 2018, www.theguardian.com/uk-news/2018/ aug/12/welsh-rail-rhondda-tunnel-could-reopen-two-mile-walk-cycle-route; Nadeem Badshah, Builders Lift the Lid on Europe's Longest Cycle Tunnel in Wales, *The Times*, 8 May 2018, www.thetimes.co.uk/article/builders-lift-the-lid-on-europes-longest-cycle-tunnel-in-wales-prg6s82rn?shareToken=c613557 315507ae2d01a4833f9a81c2b.

17 To illustrate, a simple Facebook search using the term 'Rhondda' brings up a myriad of organisations, www.facebook.com/search/str/rhondda/keywords_ search?epa=SEARCH_BOX.

18 Caton et al., 2015 (online bibliography); Kreiss et al., 2018; Joey D'Urso, Revealed: Advice to Tory MPs on How to Be 'Real' on Instagram, *BBC News Online*, 11 May 2018, www.bbc.co.uk/news/uk-politics-44047859; Hannah Murphy and Demetri Sevastopulo, Political 'Rock Stars' Woo Instagram Generation, *Finan-cial Times*, 23–24 February 2019, 4; Gaby Hinsliff, How Instagram Became the Politicians' Playground, *Observer*, 10 March 2019, www.theguardian.com/ technology/2019/mar/10/how-instagram-became-the-politicians-playground; Intimidation in Public Life: A Review by the Committee of Standards in Public Life, 13 December 2017, www.gov.uk/government/publications/intimidation-

in-public-life-a-review-by-the-committee-on-standards-in-public-life; Laura Hazard Owen, Angry Face; Facebook: Rage Now Trumps Love in Response to Legislators Facebook Posts, *NiemanLab*, 20 July 2018, www.niemanlab. org/2018/07/angry-face-facebook-rage-now-trumps-love-in-reactions-to-legisla tors-facebook-posts/?utm_source=Daily+Lab+email+list&utm_campaign= 2a361667db-dailylabemail3&utm_medium=email&utm_term=0_d68264fd5e-2a361667db-396076061.

19 Losse, 202: 149–155.
20 Annual Population Survey Estimates of Persons Aged 3 and Over Who Say They Can Speak Welsh by Local Authority and Measure, *StatsWales*, 20 September 2018, https://statswales.gov.wales/Catalogue/Welsh-Language/annualpopulation surveyestimatesofpersonsaged3andoverwhosaytheycanspeakwelsh-by-local authority-measure; responses by Robert Jones, Chris Williams and Sion Jobbins to a questionnaire, October 2018.
21 See, for example, Honeycutt and Cunliffe, 2010.
22 Mark Zuckerberg quotation comes from the Facebook Second Quarter 2018 Results Conference Call, 25 July 2018, 3, https://s21.q4cdn.com/399680738/files/ doc_financials/2018/Q2/Q218-earnings-call-transcript.pdf; Sarah Perez, Facebook Is Launching a New Groups Tab and Plug-In, *Techcrunch*, 1 May 2018, https://tech crunch.com/2018/05/01/facebook-is-launching-a-new-groups-tab-and-plugin/.
23 Stop the Great HSBC Graduate Rip-Off!!! www.facebook.com/groups/237112 2959/about/; Twitter direct message from Wes Streeting MP to the author, 21 January 2019; Dominic Rushe, Zuckerberg's Testimony: CEO Will Defend Facebook as 'Positive Force', *Guardian*, 9 April 2018, www.theguardian.com/ us-news/2018/apr/09/mark-zuckerberg-facebook-testimony-congress; on Haiti, Zuckerberg, R, 2013.
24 Hillary Clinton, Remarks on Internet Freedom, Washington, DC, 21 January 2010, archived at https://2009-2017.state.gov/secretary/20092013clinton/rm/ 2010/01/135519.htm.
25 On the anti-FARC movement, Kirkpatrick, 2011: 4–6; Zuckerberg, R, 2013; Hannes Grassegger, Facebook Says Its 'Voter Button' Is Good for Turnout: But Should the Tech Giant Be Nudging Us at All? *Observer*, 15 April 2018, 20–23; CNN interview with Wael Ghonim, 11 February 2011, www.youtube.com/ watch?v=JS4-d_Edius; Margetts et al., 2016; Tufekci, 2017.
26 Maeve Shearlaw, Five Years On: Was It Ever a 'Social Revolution', *Guardian*, 25 January 2016, www.theguardian.com/world/2016/jan/25/egypt-5-years-on-was-it-ever-a-social-media-revolution.
27 On Facebook's deactivation of the 'We Are All Khaled Said' page, see Tufekci, 2017.
28 Papacharissi, 2015; Williams, 1961.
29 The relevant Facebook pages are: We Are All Khaled Said, www.facebook. com/pg/elshaheed.co.uk/notes/?ref=page_internal   @elshaheed, www.face book.com/pg/ElShaheeed/notes/?ref=page_internal; see also The story of 'We Are All Khaled Said' Facebook Page, 26 January 2012, www.elshaheeed. co.uk/2012/01/26/the-story-of-we-are-all-khaled-said-english-faccbook-page-1-of/ and 'frenchman', History of the Revolution on Facebook, *Daily Kos*, 17 February 2011, www.dailykos.com/stories/2011/02/17/946150/-History-of-the-Revolution-on-Facebook; Margetts et al., 2016: 16; for Wael Ghonim's more recent view, see How the World Was Trolled, *Economist*, 4 November 2017, 21, also Wael Ghonim and Jake Rashbass, It's Time to End the Secrecy and

Opacity of Social Media, *Washington Post*, 31 October 2017, www.washing
tonpost.com/news/democracy-post/wp/2017/10/31/its-time-to-end-the-secrecy-
and-opacity-of-social-media/?utm_term=.9b976259db0e also see Vaidhyanathan,
127–134; My Stealthy Freedom, www.facebook.com/StealthyFreedom/; Pranav
Dixit, Meet the Women Who Have to Sneak on to Facebook, *Buzzfeed*, 8 January
2019, www.buzzfeednews.com/article/pranavdixit/facebook-women-undercover-
india.

30 Cade Metz, The Inside Story of How Facebook Is Transforming Disaster
Response, *Wired*, 10 November 2016; on the Ice Bucket Challenge, see Vaidhyanathan,
2018: 77, Margetts et al., 2016: 136–137, Facebook Newsroom, The Ice Bucket
Challenge on Facebook, 18 August 2014, updated 7 September 2014, https://
newsroom.fb.com/news/2014/08/the-ice-bucket-challenge-on-facebook/.

31 Van Dijck, 2013: 47; boyd, 2014: 201; Galloway, 2017: 177; Taplin, 2017;
Papacharissi, 2015: 9, 112. Zuckerberg, R, 2013; Losse, 2012: 41. For academic
commentary, see, for example, Tufekci, 2008; Papacharissi, 2011, 2015, 2018; van
Dijck, 2013; Simanowski, 2018: xiv, 5.

32 boyd, 2014; Monica Anderson, Skye Toor, Lee Rainie and Aaron Smith, Public Attitudes Toward Engagement on Social Media, *Per Research Center*,
11 July 2018, www.pewinternet.org/2018/07/11/public-attitudes-toward-political-
engagement-on-social-media/; Dr Frances Ryan, The Missing Link: Why Disa-
bled People Can't Afford to #deletefacebook, *Guardian*, 4 April 2018, www.
theguardian.com/media/2018/apr/04/missing-link-why-disabled-people-cant-
afford-delete-facebook-social-media?CMP=Share_iOSApp_Other.

33 Gillian Tett, Recalculating GDP for the Facebook Age, *Financial Times*,
21 November 2018, www.ft.com/content/93ffec82-ed2a-11e8-8180-9cf212677a57.

4 The Facebook system

Doing a bit of Facebookery. I could see how people get hooked.
— Alastair Campbell, February 2009[1]

Institutions matter. They have their own rules, behavioural norms, expectations of participants and sanctions against non-conforming behaviour, both formal and informal, which regulate internal conduct. Often, they have legal, financial, organisational and discursive capacities. They have operating procedures which govern their conduct and survival. These ordinarily develop over time and are codified and set down, modified by agreement or de facto by habit and routine. We can refer to these institutional rules and customs as a 'system'. Facebook has developed its own system over time. But as an institution, Facebook is reliant on *seven* particular interlocking elements which determine its growth and development. They also circumscribe the agency of Facebook users. These elements are the *seven* 'A's: architecture; advertising; accumulation; algorithms; attention; addiction; amplification. Understanding how the Facebook system works is crucial to addressing its challenges. As Siva Vaidhyanathan says,

> Facebook's surveillance system is part of its pleasure system. They cannot be severed.[2]

Architecture

Facebook's 'storytelling infrastructure', says Zizi Papacharissi, enables people to place themselves at the centre of developing world events. She suggests that 'affective attunement through liking a post on Facebook' is 'indicative of civic intensity and thus a form of engagement' even if it falls short of a deliberative ideal. Adapting Raymond Williams's 1961 concept of a 'structure of feeling', she says that social media architectures support structures of feeling 'that are affectively felt and lived prior to, or perhaps in lieu of, being ideologically articulated.'

This 'architecture of affect' – or what Karin Wahl-Jorgensen calls 'emotional architecture' – structures user-interaction with Facebook. Researchers for the Norwegian Consumer Council extensively analysed the way in which Facebook's system is designed to nudge or push users to certain courses of action:

> In Facebook's GDPR-popup, the interface was designed with a bright blue button enticing the users to 'Agree and continue'.

By contrast:

> users who wanted to limit the data Facebook collects and how they use it, had to first click a grey box labelled 'Manage data settings', where they were led through a long series of clicks.

These are deliberate architectural design choices. Taken together, Facebook's architectural design routes constitute 'a dark pattern'. Consumer organisations in the United States and the UK found similar issues.[3]

Alice Marwick and danah boyd say that social media collapses private-public boundaries. Facebook's architecture is designed to maximise user participation for revenue optimisation on and within Facebook's platform. It is designed to encourage connecting, suggesting new contacts to users ('People You May Know'), prompting people on the anniversaries of their engagement with Facebook, getting people liking, commenting and sharing.[4]

The Like button, launched on Facebook in 2009 and across the web in 2010, is a key element in generating data for Facebook both within and outside its walled garden. Wahl-Jorgensen has explored the development of Facebook's Like button – originally to be called the 'Awesome button'– and its reactions emoji. Despite support from a petition of three million users, the notion of a dislike button was rejected by Facebook, as it would have undermined 'the positive and pro-social forms of engagement' on the network. Facebook has introduced users to the concept of 'liking', leading to what has been called the 'like economy' as well as 'friending' and 'sharing'. As Zenyep Tufekci says, 'design choices constrain and structure sociality'.[5]

Advertising

Facebook offers a free service in exchange for people's data and their attention, which enables Facebook to charge advertisers for user engagement. Facebook has said it never sells users' data, but the release of Facebook e-mails as a result of leaks of evidence from the Six4Three court case in California led the House of Commons DCMS Select Committee to say in 2019:

> We consider that data transfer for value is Facebook's business model and that Mark Zuckerberg's statement that 'we've never sold anyone's data' is simply untrue.

Further emails released show that Facebook conceived a 'dollars for data' programme and that Zuckerberg thought of Facebook as an information 'bank'. These issues have been contested by Facebook.[6]

Facebook's advertising model has developed over time but only became turbo-charged in the period around its IPO in 2012. Facebook moved rapidly to work out how to link data from different sources, including from data brokers, in a way that was valuable to advertisers and also political campaigns.[7]

Facebook advertising is based on the programmatic advertising model which has evolved over the last twenty years. Mark Zuckerberg told the Senate,

> we basically calculate on – on our side which ads are going to be relevant for people, and we have an incentive to show people ads that are going to be relevant because we only get paid when it delivers a business result, and – and that's how the system works . . . we get paid when the action of the advertiser wants to – to happen, happens.

The majority of online advertising is now sold through automated real-time 'programmatic advertising' or 'behavioural targeting'.

Many advertisers may be bidding for access to an individual as they land on a website. An advertising exchange consists of Supply Side Platforms (SSP) and Demand Side Platforms (DSP). Publishers make their content available to advertising exchanges via the SSP. Advertisers decide which audiences they wish to target via the DSP. An individual visits a webpage. As it loads, information about the individual and the content of the page is gathered and reported back to the ad exchange. Algorithms process the information, and the advertiser is entered into an auction with other advertisers also bidding for the individual. Publishers get paid for the content shown on their sites. This all happens in milliseconds.[8]

Facebook's advertising system is

> a complex model that considers both the dollar value of each bid as well as how good a piece of clickbait (or view-bait, or comment-bait) the corresponding ad is. If Facebook's model thinks your ad is 10 times more likely to engage a user than another company's ad, then your effective bid at auction is considered 10 times higher than a company willing to pay the same dollar amount.[9]

At the time of its IPO, Facebook's 'like' and 'share' buttons were on half of all US websites. The system also serves ads into Instagram and now Facebook Messenger. Facebook ads are known as 'promoted' or 'sponsored' content – they will often include a note that your friends have liked a specific page or item and possibly ask you to like as well, which may mean content from that site subsequently appearing in your News Feed without being sponsored.

Facebook allows advertisers to micro-target an audience based on 98 or so characteristics including demographics, location, interests and behaviours, including purchasing and device usage. In Congress, Zuckerberg was vague about this. Facebook may use up to 52,000 different attributes to categorise Facebook users, provide some 29,000 categories on Facebook users to ad buyers and hold 1,500 data points on average on non-Facebook users. Challenged if he could confirm these figures in his hearing in the House of Representatives, Mark Zuckerberg said, 'I do not know off the top of my head'.[10]

Facebook advertising tools have been simply explained by the UK Information Commissioner (ICO).[11] In summary,

Custom Audiences are created using data about an individual which an advertiser already possesses, which is then matched with Facebook data.

Lookalike audiences are created on the basis of an existing Custom audience, whose characteristics are used by advertisers to create a larger group who share the same attributes.

Partner categories allows advertisers to draw on data supplied by third-party organisations such as data brokers to help them target users.

The *Facebook Audience Network* consists of Facebook advertisers seeking to expand their advertising across the web and in apps. Facebook offers a variety of advertising formats designed to fit advertisers' content, including 'native' advertising which matches the look and style of the app or site where they appear. This 'blurs the line' between editorial and advertising.

Facebook *Pixels* are pieces of code or 'cookies' placed on websites to register when Facebook users visit it. Facebook allows advertisers to target users who had visited a specific website.[12] Facebook is now adding the pixel to Facebook Groups.[13]

When he launched Facebook advertising back in 2007, Zuckerberg said,

Nothing influences people more than a recommendation from a trusted friend. A trusted referral is the Holy Grail of advertising.[14]

Research suggests that users don't know how advertising is targeted to them, and some do not understand how platforms make their money. For a long time, Facebook has been judge and jury on its own advertising statistics, whereas newspaper, radio and television advertising has long been independently audited.[15]

The development of personalised advertising has led to social discrimination. Facebook has allowed racially targeted advertising: it is being taken to court by the Housing and Urban Development authority in the United States for racial discrimination in its advertising and has had to reach a settlement with Washington State.[16]

Accumulation

In March 2018, the *Observer* and *Channel 4* in the UK and the *New York Times* revealed the extent of Facebook user data obtained by the London-based voter targeting company Cambridge Analytica. The UK ICO has said that her team were working through 700 terabytes of data from Cambridge Analytica, and the investigation is the largest ever undertaken in the world by a data protection authority.[17]

Facebook is subject to a consent order made by the Federal Trade Commission (FTC) between 2011 and 2012, following various consumer data issues. The FTC said Facebook was a company 'whose entire business model rests on collecting, maintaining, and sharing people's information' and imposed 20 years of privacy audits on the company. The UK House of Commons DCMS Select Committee has said that if Facebook had fully complied with the FTC order, then the subsequent Cambridge Analytica scandal would not have happened. In April 2019, Facebook said it had set aside billions in case of an FTC fine.[18]

Cambridge Analytica's parent company, SCL, had developed a relationship with a former Cambridge University researcher, Dr Aleksandr Kogan, and his app ('Thisisyourdigitallife') developed through his company GSR. The ICO said, 'The app featured a personality test, and it was in relation to this that Dr Kogan entered into a contract with SCL Elections Ltd by which the latter would pay for US citizens to take the test'.

Three hundred and twenty thousand Facebook users were paid to take a detailed online personality test developed by Kogan. The test gathered users' data and also data from their friends. The data of some 87 million people was accessed as a result, 70 million of them in the United States. For 30 million Facebook users, concluded the ICO, 'the personality test results were paired with Facebook data to seek out psychological patterns and build models'. The personality test profiled people against five scales of the 'OCEAN' model: openness to experience, conscientiousness, extraversion, agreeableness and neuroticism. It is believed Cambridge Analytica then combined this with other sources of data, such as voter records held by SCL, to help inform targeting of individuals in key marginal US states with personalised advertising during the presidential election process. At the time of writing in April 2019, more detail keeps emerging, with a report from the Canadian Privacy Commissioner the latest example, but the full facts must await the end of the UK ICO inquiry in late 2019.[19]

Kogan had developed his app after working in the same department where Michael Kosinski and colleagues had previously identified how it was possible to understand key personality traits of individuals by analysing their Facebook likes. Facebook subsequently suspended the MyPersonality app on which the Kosinski research had been developed.[20] Kogan shared some of the data accessed from Facebook with others, including a company called Euonia Technologies, founded by Christopher Wylie, who subsequently came to be the whistleblower who provided information to the *Observer*'s Carole Cadwalladr.

Kogan was able to develop his app as a result of Facebook's platform strategy. In 2008, Facebook launched version 1 of its Graph Application Platform Interface (API). This allowed app developers to access Facebook data concerning Facebook users and their friends. According to the ICO, 'Facebook did not take sufficient steps to prevent apps from collecting data in contravention of data protection law'.

Facebook made changes to its developer platform in 2014 after an audit by the Irish Data Protection Commissioner, as the lead European data protection authority for Facebook, which reduced the ability of apps to access information about their users and about the Facebook friends of their users. There was a one-year grace period until May 2015 for some of these apps. The Information Commissioner said, 'it was during this grace period that the GSR app accessed the majority of its information'.

In December 2015, the *Guardian* newspaper ran an extensive article about the Ted Cruz campaign and how it was using 'pyschographics' developed by Cambridge Analytica, based on Facebook data that might have been harvested from Facebook users without their permission. Facebook asked Cambridge Analytica to delete the data that it held and any derivative data. Facebook undertook no forensic checks to ensure that deletion had taken place, and the ICO has said that Facebook's actions were 'ineffective and slow'. Mark Zuckerberg has publicly said that he did not know Cambridge Analytica had failed to delete the data until the stories broke in March 2018. Challenged in the US Senate, Zuckerberg appeared unaware that Kogan's terms of service allowed him to sell the data he collected.[21]

Kogan told the Senate he had made Facebook aware in the Spring of 2015. Who in Facebook knew what and when is under scrutiny in a Washington,

DC, court, where the district attorney-general has filed suit against Facebook. The UK ICO has said that senior people in Facebook were aware of the data breach 'in 2014–15'. She did not have evidence that Mark Zuckerberg knew, but 'that is not to say that he did not know'. Facebook had also employed Kogan's former GSR partner, Joseph Chancellor, as a virtual reality researcher in 2015 until it confirmed in September 2018 that he no longer worked for the company. Zuckerberg says Facebook may sue Kogan. Kogan is now suing Facebook.[22]

The House of Commons DCMS Select Committee has said 'it was a profound failure of governance within Facebook' that the matter wasn't immediately referred to Mark Zuckerberg in 2015. The Information Commissioner issued its maximum possible fine of £500,000 to Facebook in October 2018, because of Facebook's 'repeated failures' to protect users' data. At least one million UK users had been put at risk. The Information Commissioner, Elizabeth Denham, had previously been acting Privacy Commissioner in Canada, where she had carried out a previous inquiry into Facebook in 2008, 'which laid bare the business model of Facebook'. Ms Denham said that she felt that Facebook 'has looked at the Canadian finding and the Canadian and Irish recommendations more as advice'. Facebook would not change its business model without a legal order compelling it to do so.[23]

Facebook has also purchased data from data brokers to supplement Facebook data to target Facebook users, though in March 2018, Facebook said it would no longer do this. They would be shutting down Facebook Partner Categories. Facebook has sought to give the impression that it was GDPR-compliant – even that it considered GDPR a possible gold standard for data protection globally. The Irish DPC said at the end of 2018 it is currently examining ten possible breaches of GDPR by Facebook.[24]

In his House of Representatives' hearing in April 2018, Congressman Lujan asked Mark Zuckerberg about the collection of data on non-Facebook users:

LUJAN: So these are called shadow profiles? Is that what they've been referred to by some?
ZUCKERBERG: Congressman, I'm not – I'm not familiar with that . . .

In fact, Facebook had called these 'dark profiles'. Former Facebook employee Kate Losse says that Facebook's product team created 'dark profiles' in the autumn of 2006: hidden profiles of people who were not yet on Facebook but whose photographs had been tagged on the site. Facebook subsequently said, 'We do not create profiles for non-Facebook users, nor do we use browser and app logs for non-Facebook users to show targeted ads from our advertisers to them or otherwise seek to personalize the content they see'. That leaves open the question of whether they had done so in the past.[25]

Mark Zuckerberg told the Senate in April 2018 that he could technically look at a user's file 'but it would be a massive breach'. Losse says that Facebook employees who had 'super access' – the facility to view anyone's data regardless of privacy settings – never wanted to lose it. According to a report from security journalist Brian Krebs in March 2019, Facebook stored 600 million user account passwords without encryption and viewable as plain text by 20,000 company employees. Both of these matters are serious issues: under GDPR, shadow profiles are likely to be illegal, and storing user passwords in plain text with mass access is likely to be a major breach of basic rules on data storage.[26]

Since the Cambridge Analytica scandal, journalists have been very alive to further Facebook data issues. Facebook is reportedly under criminal investigation over data-sharing with device manufacturers. The SEC and the judiciary department are looking into its data issues as is the FTC. Among potentially the most serious issues was the April 2019 disclosure that Facebook may have harvested 1.5 million users' email contacts, now under investigation in Europe as well. Losse says, 'At Facebook, you had to always assume surveillance, as that was our business'.[27]

Algorithms

In March 2019, Facebook began to explain to users how News Feed worked, in a feature it planned to roll out worldwide. Research shows that most people do not understand how the News Feed operates. Facebook's algorithms have been extensively analysed by Taina Bucher: Edgerank (as it was known then) judged every interaction a user makes, and Graphrank sifted these for meaningful patterns. Facebook algorithms rank objects (e.g., photographs), the user and what Facebook calls 'edges' – interactions. There are a number of elements to this ranking: the available range of stories; the data points or signals that can inform ranking decisions; the predictions which Facebook makes, based on what it knows about you, as to how likely you are to engage with a story, liking, commenting or sharing it with friends, hide it or mark it as spam; and a score for the relevancy of that story to you. Time decay – i.e., the length of time between postings – is also a factor. Sharing an item was worth more than commenting, and commenting worth more than liking.[28]

The legal scholar Karen Yeung argues that what we are seeing today is a process of algorithmic 'nudges' which shape user choices 'through processes that are subtle, unobtrusive yet extraordinarily powerful'. The News Feed, say Parker et al. 'is a classic multiuser feedback loop'. The average user has access to about 1,500 posts daily, but Facebook estimates that we see about 10% of everything posted by our friends and other organisations with whom we have engaged. Instagram moved from a chronologically sorted to an algorithmically organised feed in 2016.[29]

After Facebook was forced to give evidence to Congress in 2017 about the impact of Russian advertising and fake news, the company announced further changes to News Feed in January 2018. These were designed to ensure that 'meaningful social interactions' were prioritised: users were likely to see fewer stories from news organisations. Facebook wanted to prioritise friends and family. This was not a new claim. In making changes to the News Feed in June 2016, Facebook said, 'Today, we're announcing an update to News Feed that helps you see more posts from your friends and family'. They admitted then, 'we do this not only because we believe it's the right thing but also because it's good for our business'.[30]

A simpler algorithm drives the nudges to connect with new people on Facebook, known as the 'People You May Know' feature. This has on occasions proved controversial with users. It has surfaced abusive partners, estranged relatives, patients of doctors, sperm donors and their offspring, sex workers and clients amongst others and friends who have passed away. The UK Online Harms White Paper suggests giving an online regulator the right to test and inspect algorithms.[31]

Attention

Social media have given us an ever-increasing flow of information, from the latest uploaded family photographs to entertaining videos about domestic animals to news gobbets designed to shape outraged reactions. Attention is a scarce commodity. The commercial battle for our attention is not a new one, as Tim Wu explains, arguing that 'advertising was the conversion engine that, with astonishing efficiency, turned the cash crop of attention into an industrial commodity'. Facebook, with more data than most, can afford to run thousands of experiments to assess the effectiveness of its attempts to keep us locked in its system.

This is not, of course, accidental. This attention economy developed an intensity in the 1990s once Silicon Valley's surveillance capitalism demanded that new digital services supplying content should be free to users, as this dictated that advertising based on data-mining would be the dominant revenue source. Web-based and subsequently app-based technologies offered new opportunities for advertisers who began to move away from brand-building to targeting. At Silicon Valley's Stanford University, there is even a Persuasive Technology Laboratory, where the study of what is called 'captology' is undertaken to find ways of making people click more and remain within an app universe. Advertisers are concerned about 'dwell time'.[32]

Facebook's growth team, 'aggressively focused on engagement', has become extraordinarily good at managing the attention economy, finding ways to bring people onto the platform and keep them there, developing the new metrics of engagement – for example, monthly active users – in a practice called 'growth accounting'. They also developed the 'People You May Know' feature. Another example is the Facebook notification icon: originally blue, it was changed to red when no one used it, according to former Google manager Tristan Harris, founder of *Time Well Spent*: red, he says, 'is a trigger colour', explaining why it is used as an alarm signal. This inevitably has been accelerated by the smartphone, always on and always connected to the web.[33]

Addiction

In her analysis of the use of social media by teenagers, danah boyd notes that new technologies often provoke moral panics about their supposed dangers. She notes that some do come to form an unhealthy relationship with smartphones and apps, in terms of what might be called 'behavioural compulsions'. She also notes how people speak 'jocularly' about their addiction to social media. She is right to stress that the dangers of 'addiction' and behavioural compulsion can be over-stated. However, an increasing number of scientists are now raising questions about the engineered addictive qualities of social media: 'legalised crack', as Martinez calls it. One study suggested just seeing the Facebook logo can provoke a craving for social media. Infamously, Facebook ran an experiment in 2014 alongside Cornell University that demonstrated the company's ability to influence emotional responses positively or negatively.

Respected psychologists and neuroscientists state that Facebook encourages the release of dopamine into the brain, an organic chemical associated with pleasurable feelings. By posting pleasurable messages, we are also seeking to raise the level of Oxycontin in respondents so that they like what we have posted. This helps raise our sense of esteem. Whether or not this is a matter of addiction, defined as a state of dependence, remains contested, but these features are designed into social media such as Facebook. Some argue that the appeal of social networking is rooted in biological urges which we may not understand. Prominent former Facebook employees and advisers have also weighed in against Facebook's dopamine-driven behavioural toxicity. Roger McNamee says this is a public health crisis: he is particularly scathing about the creation of Messenger Kids, launched in 2017, against the advice of many child health experts. Several of those who vetted it had been funded by Facebook.[34]

The interaction of young people with social media has become a signifi-cant, but arguably under-researched, area of public policy. Although plat-forms such as Facebook have an age limit of 13, restricting when young people can join, research has shown that many children younger than 13 do access social media.[35] The use of '13' as an age limit derives from the Children's Online Privacy Protection Act of 1998 in the United States, which pre-dates the creation of major social networks like Facebook. John Carr, Secretary of the UK Children's Charities Coalition on Internet Safety and adviser to the Internet Watch Foundation, says that the age limit of 13 has not been properly researched and that when the European Union was adopting the GDPR, the original proposed single EU-wide age limit of 13 was instead converted at the last minute into a range from 13 to 16, with individual member states left free to choose: a variety of age limits now exist. Social psychologist Sonia Livingstone, who is leading a significant research project on children's data and privacy online, points out that chil-dren's voices are 'particularly absent' from national or international delib-erations on online issues. With time spent by young people online doubling over the last decade, this has become an area of increasing controversy, but research has produced mixed results, suggesting correlation but not neces-sarily causation of harm to mental health. But most would advocate taking a precautionary approach, and the ICO has launched a Code of Practice to protect children and young people online, setting out standards for age-appropriate design for online services, with privacy by default settings. This is scarcely surprising, given that Facebook executives have marketed the ability of their service to identify when teenagers feel insecure or worthless or need a confidence boost and therefore are most susceptible to particular kinds of marketing.[36]

Amplification

On 15 November 2018, Mark Zuckerberg posted a 5,000-word essay on his Facebook page where he confirmed something that had been known by researchers for years but which had been downplayed in Facebook statements and corporate actions: Facebook's algorithm prioritised posts which were controversial, resulting in 'polarization and extremism'. Zuckerberg said, 'when left unchecked, people will engage dispropor-tionately with more sensationalist and provocative content'. Facebook research showed that, no matter where the line was drawn, as a piece of content got closer to the prohibited line, people would engage with it more, even if they didn't like it. Facebook amplifies extreme and polaris-ing content and views.[37]

Zuckerberg said Facebook could address this by 'penalizing borderline content so it gets less distribution and engagement'. To do that, Facebook would change its News Feed algorithm and its other 'recommendation systems'. This would depend on developing better-trained artificial intelligence systems. While this would address many challenges, it also reinforces Facebook's power, meaning that much inflammatory content will disappear without Facebook having to account for why it has been taken down.[38]

danah boyd says Facebook and other social networks provide new affordances 'for amplifying, recording and spreading information and social acts'. Facebook has been used in a systematic way by a range of extremist organisations to recruit new members by leading them through a process of engagement, whereby more and more extreme content is recommended to them.

Renee DiResta, head of policy at Data for Democracy, writes of how extremists develop their views:

> They usually report that their initial exposure started with a question, and that a search engine took them to content that they found compelling. They engaged with the content and then found more. They joined a few groups, and soon a recommendation engine sent them others.[39]

Academic research has shown how conspiracy theories spread fast on Facebook and other platforms and how some groups may be more prone to believing conspiracy theories, fake news, disinformation and so on. Fact-checking has no impact on these groups. As DiResta notes,

> When Facebook tried adding fact-checking to misinformation, researchers found, counterintuitively, that people doubled down and shared the article more when it was disputed. They don't want you to know, readers claimed, alleging that Facebook was trying to censor controversial knowledge.

Disturbingly, Facebook's increasing focus on Groups could increase the effect of amplification of polarising and extreme material, feeding what the legal scholar Cass Sunstein calls 'the law of group polarization'.[40]

The amplification effect of social media has also been cited in respect of young people and depression, with the tragedy in the UK in 2017 of the young teenager Molly Russell, who took her own life after searching for images of self-harm on social media. It transpired that her Instagram feed was full of such materials. Following a public outcry in the UK, with calls from the Secretary of State for Health for real action by platforms, Instagram announced it was going to pull graphic images of self-harm. Images of anorexia also thrive on the platform.[41] The problem is that recommendation engines on Facebook and Instagram and other social media can keep amplifying more and more extreme material to people. Perhaps it is no wonder that Facebook has embarked on an advertising campaign to explain how they have made a tool for people to judge how long they are spending online.

Notes

1 Campbell, 2018.
2 Vaidhyanathan, 2018: 51.
3 Papacharissi, 2015; Wahl-Jorgensen, 2018a and 2018b; Deceived by Design, *Norwegian Consumer Council*, 27 June 2018, https://fil.forbrukerradet.no/wp-content/uploads/2018/06/2018-06-27-deceived-by-design-final.pdf; CU letter to FTC on Norwegian Consumer Council Report 'Deceived by Design' and CU Research on Facebook and Google Sign-Up, 27 June 2018, https://advocacy.consumerreports.org/research/letter-to-ftc-norwegian-consumer-council-report-deceived-by-design/; How to Manage Your Facebook Data and Manage Targeted Ads, *Which*, n.d., www.which.co.uk/consumer-rights/advice/how-to-manage-your-facebook-data-and-manage-targeted-ads.
4 Marwick and boyd, 2014; Gerlitz and Helmond, 2013; Bucher, 2012.
5 Wahl-Jorgensen, 2018a, 2018b; on liking, see Wagner, 2018: 231; on the like economy, Gerlitz and Helmond, 2013; on friending, Zuckerberg, R, 2015; on sharing, John, 2012; Tufekci, 2010.
6 Deepa Seetharaman and Kirsten Grind, Facebook Considered Charging for Access to User Data, *Wall Street Journal*, 28 November 2018, www.wsj.com/articles/facebook-considered-charging-for-access-to-user-data-1543454648; House of Commons, 2019b. Bill Goodwin, Sebastian Klovig Skelton and Duncan Campbell, Facebook Leaks: Zuckerberg Turned Data into Dollars in Ruthless Battle with Competitors, *Computer Weekly*, 18 April 2019, www.computerweekly.com/news/252461895/Facebook-leaks-Zuckerberg-turned-data-into-dollars-in-ruthless-battle-with-competitors.
7 Martinez, 2016: 4–5; Kreiss, 2017.
8 *Washington Post*, 2018a; Nairn, 2018; House of Lords, 2018b; Turow, 2012.
9 Antonio Garcia Martinez, How Trump Conquered Facebook – Without Russian Ads, *Wired*, 23 February 2018, www.wired.com/story/how-trump-conquered-facebookwithout-russian-ads/.
10 Caitlin Dewey, 98 Personal Data Points That Facebook Uses to Target Ads to You, *Washington Post*, 29 August 2016, www.washingtonpost.com/news/the-intersect/wp/2016/08/19/98-personal-data-points-that-facebook-uses-to-target-ads-to-you/?utm_term=.f5fdd08c7e54; Hard Questions: What Data Does Facebook Collect When I'm Not on Facebook, and Why? *Facebook Newsroom*, 16 April 2018, https://newsroom.fb.com/news/2018/04/data-off-facebook/; *Washington Post*, 2018a. Julia Angwin, Surya Mattu and Terry Parris Jr., Facebook Doesn't Tell Users Everything It Really Knows About Them, *ProPublica*, 27 December 2016, www.propublica.org/article/facebook-doesnt-tell-users-everything-it-really-knows-about-them; House of Representatives, 2018.
11 ICO, 2018b.
12 Audience Network by Facebook, n.d., www.facebook.com/audiencenetwork/products/overview; House of Commons 2019b, paragraph 181.

13 Kerry Flynn, Facebook Adds Pixel to Groups So Marketers Can Track Engaged Audiences, *Digiday*, 27 August 2018, https://digiday.com/marketing/facebook-adds-pixel-groups-marketers-can-track-engaged-audiences/.

14 Facebook Unveils Facebook Ads, *Facebook Newsroom*, 6 November 2007, https://newsroom.fb.com/news/2007/11/facebook-unveils-facebook-ads/.

15 Doteveryone, People Power and Technology: The 2018 Digital Understanding Report, http://understanding.doteveryone.org.uk; Jason Kint: Here Are 5 Ways Facebook Violates Consumer Expectations to Maximise Its Profits, 10 April 2018, www.niemanlab.org/2018/04/jason-kint-here-are-5-ways-facebook-violates-consumer-expectations-to-maximize-its-profits/; Facebook took down 2.2 billion fake accounts in the first quarter of 2019 – the same number as it has users: Daniel Howley, Facebook Says It Took Down 2.2 Billion Fake Accounts in 2019, *Yahoo Finance*, 23 May 2019, https://finance.yahoo.com/news/facebook-fake-accounts-174616111.html?guccounter=1&guce_referrer=aHR0cHM6L y9kdWNrZHVja2dvLmNvbS8&guce_referrer_sig=AQAAAKf8nwgse0Jlq 06YQuk5dOdGxgbGZ_g_DKlSw8YRYhLxwgwXbkMMSo-knpRDNGR_gA8GxUphVKiRD8iBd3cWspejensF6fafxlmVIByg9g0S3Zt-yHvXGFoUSU WmrRFOlpiu_xMYu73ULONNflAph1BsEYIr-_AP0Yh3lc4kgF5R; Ad Fraud Is Estimated at Between $6.5 Million and $16.5 Billion Per Annum: Nairn, 2018.

16 On personalised advertising and social discrimination, Turow, 2012; Lynskey, 2018; Ariana Tobin, HUD Sues Facebook Over Housing Discrimination and Says the Company's Algorithms Have Made the Problem Worse, *ProPublica*, 28 March 2019, www.propublica.org/article/hud-sues-facebook-housing-dis crimination-advertising-algorithms; Tom Knowles, Facebook Let Advertisers Seek Out Nazi Sympathisers, *The Times*, 23 February 2019, 37. Turow, 2012. AG Ferguson Investigation Leads to Facebook Making Nationwide Changes to Prohibit Discriminatory Advertisements on Its Platform, Office of the Attorney-General, *Washington State*, 24 July 2018, www.atg.wa.gov/news/news-releases/ag-ferguson-investigation-leads-facebook-making-nationwide-changes-prohibit.

17 International Grand Committee, Oral Evidence, 27 November 2018 (evidence from Elizabeth Denham, Information Commissioner).

18 FTC, 2012; Facebook, 2019b; On Facebook privacy see amongst others, Tufekci, 2008; Papacharissi, 2010; Van Dijck, 2013; Vaidhyanathan, 2018.

19 Facebook refuses to address serious privacy deficiencies despite public apologies for 'breach of trust', Office of the Privacy Commissioner of Canada, 25 April 2019, www.priv.gc.ca/en/opc-news/news-and-announcements/2019/nr-c_190425/.

20 Kosinski et al., 2013; Youyou et al., 2015.

21 DPC, 2011, 2012; Information Commissioner's Office, 2018a, 2018b, 2018c; Harry Davies, Ted Cruz Using Firm That Harvested Data on Millions of Unwitting Facebook Users, *Guardian*, 11 December 2015, www.theguardian.com/us-news/2015/dec/11/senator-ted-cruz-president-campaign-facebook-user-data; Your Facebook data has probably already been scraped, Mark Zuckerberg says, Kif Leswing, *Business Insider*, 5 April 2018, www.businessinsider.sg/mark-zuckerberg-april-2018-conference-call-on-facebook-privacy-full-transcript-2018-4/.

22 Paul Grewal, Suspending Cambridge Analytica and SCL Elections from Facebook, *Facebook Newsroom*, 16 March 2018, https://newsroom.fb.com/news/2018/03/suspending-cambridge-analytica/; *Washington Post*, 2018a; Complaint for Violations of the Consumer Protections Procedures Act District

of Columbia v. Facebook Inc, In the Superior Court of the District of Columbia Civil Division, https://oag.dc.gov/sites/default/files/2018-12/Facebook-Complaint_0.pdf; International Grand Committee, Oral Evidence, 27 November 2018. Donie O'Sullivan, Facebook Employee with Ties to Cambridge Analytica Leaves Company, *CNN*, 7 September 2018, https://money.cnn.com/2018/09/07/technology/facebook-cambridge-analytica-joseph-chancellor/index.html; Mathew Rosenberg, Academic Behind Cambridge Aanalytica Data-Mining Sues Facebook for Defamation, *New York Times*, 15 March 2019, www.nytimes.com/2019/03/15/technology/aleksandr-kogan-facebook-cambridge-analytica.html.

23 Carole Cadwalladr, Ice-Cool Canadian Fighting Firms Who Abuse on Data, *Observer*, 15 July 2018, 32–33; ICO, 2018d; International Grand Committee, Oral Evidence, 27 November 2018.

24 Kurt Wagner, Facebook Is Cutting Third-Party Data Providers Out of Ad Targeting to Clean Up Its Act, *Recode*, 28 March 2018, www.recode.net/2018/3/28/17174098/facebook-data-advertising-targeting-change-experian-acxiom; Recode, July 2018; Irish DPC, 2018.

25 Losse, 2012: 88; Facebook replies to Senate, June 2018, www.commerce.senate.gov/public/_cache/files/ed0185fb-615a-4fd5-818b-5ce050825a9b/62027BC70720678CBC934C93214B0871.senate-judiciary-combined-7-.pdf.

26 *Washington Post*, 2018a, 2018b; Losse, 2012: 89. Brian Krebs, Facebook Stored Hundreds of Millions of User Passwords in Plain Text for Years, *Krebs on Security*, 21 March 2019, https://krebsonsecurity.com/2019/03/facebook-stored-hundreds-of-millions-of-user-passwords-in-plain-text-for-years/. Facebook has now confirmed that millions of Instagram users were also affected: Pedro Canahuati, Keeping Passwords Secure, *Facebook Newsroom*, 21 March 2019, https://newsroom.fb.com/news/2019/03/keeping-passwords-secure/.

27 Facebook shared data with a wide variety of device manufacturers, retailers and other 'integration partners' – potentially as many as 150 – including Russian search engine Yandex, accused of 'overtly close ties to the Kremlin', according to the *New York Times* (NYT). The link to Yandex had not been secret: Reuters reported it in 2014: Russia's Yandex to Get Access to Facebook Content, *Reuters*, 14 January 2014, www.reuters.com/article/us-yandex-facebook/russias-yandex-to-get-access-to-facebook-content-idUSBREA0D0IB20140114; Jason Silverstein, Hundreds of Millions of Facebook User Records Were Exposed on Amazon Cloud Server, *CBS News*, 4 April 2019, www.cbsnews.com/news/millions-facebook-user-records-exposed-amazon-cloud-server/; Gabriel J.X. Dance, Nicholas Confessore and Michael LaForgia, Facebook Gave Device Makers Deep Access to Data on Users and Friends, *New York Times*, 3 June 2018, www.nytimes.com/interactive/2018/06/03/technology/facebook-device-partners-users-friends-data.html; Gabriel J.X. Dance, Michael LaForgia and Nicholas Confessore, As Facebook Raised a Privacy Wall, It Carved an Opening for Tech Giants, *New York Times*, 18 December 2018, www.nytimes.com/2018/12/18/technology/facebook-privacy.html; Michael LaForgia, Matthew Rosenberg and Gabriel J.X. Dance, Facebook's Data Deals Are Under Criminal Investigation, *New York Times*, 13 March 2019, www.nytimes.com/2019/03/13/technology/facebook-data-deals-investigation.html; Rob Price, An EU Government Data Watchdog Is 'Engaging' with Facebook After It Harvested 1.5 Million Users' Email Contacts Without Consent, *Business Insider*, 18 April 2019, www.businessinsider.com/ireland-dpc-agency-info-facebook-collection-1-5-million-email-contacts-2019-4?r=US&IR=T. There have been

many other incidents since the Cambridge Analytica revelations, but there is no space to list them all. Losse, 2012: 222.

28 Ramya Sethuraman, Why Am I Seeing This? We Have an Answer for You, *Facebook Newsroom*, 31 March 2019, https://newsroom.fb.com/news/2019/03/why-am-i-seeing-this/; Aaron Smith, Many Facebook Users Don't Understand How the Facebook News Feed Works, *Pew Research Center*, 5 September 2018, www.pewresearch.org/fact-tank/2018/09/05/many-facebook-users-dont-understand-how-the-sites-news-feed-works/; Bucher, 2012: 484–488; Josh Constine, How Instagram's Algorithm Works, *Techcrunch*, 1 June 2018, https://techcrunch.com/2018/06/01/how-instagram-feed-works/.

29 Yeung, 2017: 119; online bibliography: Parker et al., 2017: 46. Will Oremus, Who Controls Your Facebook Feed, *Slate*, 3 January 2016, www.slate.com/articles/technology/cover_story/2016/01/how_facebook_s_news_feed_algorithm_works.html; Ken Yeung, Facebook Says About 10% of Posts Are Read Daily, *Venture Beat*, 14 September 2016, https://venturebeat.com/2016/09/14/facebook-says-about-10-of-news-feed-stories-are-actually-read-daily/; Josh Constine, How Facebook News Feed Works, *Techcrunch*, 6 September 2016, https://techcrunch.com/2016/09/06/ultimate-guide-to-the-news-feed/; Adam Mosseri, Inside News Feed Ranking in Three Minutes Flat, *Facebook Newsroom*, 22 May 2018, https://newsroom.fb.com/news/2018/05/inside-feed-news-feed-ranking/.

30 Adam Mosseri, Building a Better News Feed for You, *Facebook Newsroom*, 29 June 2016, http://newsroom.fb.com/news/2016/06/building-a-better-news-feed-for-you/; Mark Zuckerberg, *Facebook Post*, 11 January 2018, www.facebook.com/zuck/posts/10104413015393571; Jillian D'Onfro, Facebook Is Massively Changing Its News Feed, and It May Mean People Spend Less Time on It, *CNBC*, 11 January 2018, www.cnbc.com/2018/01/11/major-change-to-facebook-news-feed-to-improve-well-being-mark-zuckerberg.html; Ben Thompson: An interview with Adam Mosseri, *Stratechery*, 16 January 2018, https://stratechery.com/2018/an-interview-with-facebook-vice-president-of-news-feed-adam-mosseri/.

31 M. J. Franklin, 'People You May Know' Is the Perfect Demonstration of Everything That's Wrong with Facebook, *Mashable*, 15 May 2018, https://mashable.com/article/people-you-may-know-facebook-creepy/?europe=true; Kashmir Hill, 'People You May Know' a Controversial Facebook Feature's 10-Year History, *Gizmodo*, 8 August 2018, https://gizmodo.com/people-you-may-know-a-controversial-facebook-features-1827981959; DCMS, 2019.

32 Wu, 2016: 9; Vaidhyanathan, 2018: 81; Owen, 2015: 197; Turow, 2012; Persuasive Tech Lab, http://captology.stanford.edu; Fogg, 2003. Mcnamee, 2019; Facebook's Dwell Time Question at Home, *Enders Analysis*, January 2018, www.endersanalysis.com/content/publication/facebooks-dwell-time-question-home; Marwick, 2015.

33 Hannah Kuchler, How Facebook Grew Too Big to Handle, *Financial Times Magazine*, 30 March 2019, www.ft.com/content/be723754-501c-11e9-9c76-bf4a0ce37d49; Paul Lewis, Our Minds Can Be Hijacked, *Guardian*, 5 October 2017, www.theguardian.com/technology/2017/oct/05/smartphone-addiction-silicon-valley-dystopia.

34 boyd, 2014; Martinez, 2016; Greenfield, 2015; McNamee, 2019; Livingstone, 2018; See Frederic Filloux, Facebook Has a Big Tobacco Problem, *Monday Note*, 12 February 2018, https://mondaynote.com/facebook-has-a-big-tobacco-problem-f801085109a; Hilary Andersson, Social Media Apps Are Deliberately Addictive to Users, 4 July 2018, www.bbc.co.uk/news/technology-44640959;

10 April 2018; former Facebook executives turning on its addictive qualities include Sean Parker, Olivia Solon, Ex-Facebook President Sean Parker: Site Made to Exploit Human Vulnerability, *Guardian*, 9 November 2017, www. theguardian.com/technology/2017/nov/09/facebook-sean-parker-vulnerabil ity-brain-psychology, former vice-president of Growth, Chamath Palihapitiya: Elizabeth Dwoskin, What Facebook's Fight with a Former Executive Says About Social Media's Future, *Washington Post*, 15 December 2017, www.washington post.com/news/the-switch/wp/2017/12/15/what-facebooks-intensely-personal-fight-with-a-former-executive-says-about-social-medias-future/?utm_term=. e9432a53effb and Sandy Parakilas, Former Product Executive: Noah Kulwin, Facebook Is a Fundamentally Addictive Product, *New York Magazine*, 10 April 2018, http://nymag.com/intelligencer/2018/04/sandy-parakilas-former-facebook-employee-interview.html; Noah Kulwin, You Have a Persuasion Engine Unlike Anything in History, *New York* magazine, http://nymag.com/intelligencer/2018/ 04/roger-mcnamee-early-facebook-investor-interview.html; Nitasha Tiku, Facebook Funded Most of the Experts Who Vetted Messenger Kids, *Wired*, 14 February 2018, www.wired.com/story/facebook-funds-its-favorite-experts-but-skirts-tough-critics/.

35 Children's Commissioner for England, Life in Likes, 4 January 2018, www. childrenscommissioner.gov.uk/2018/01/04/children-unprepared-for-social-media-cliff-edge-as-they-start-secondary-school-childrens-commissioner-for-england-warns-in-new-report/.

36 Telephone interview with John Carr, 29 March 2019; Ian Sample, Bedtime Social Media Use May Be Harming UK Teenagers, Says Study, *Guardian*, 23 February 2019, 5; Denis Campbell, NHS Urges Social Media to Ban Celebrity Ads for 'Health' Products, *Guardian*, 2 February 2019, 3. For studies of impact on children and young people, Orben and Przybylski, 2019; Frith, 2017; Livingstone et al., for UKCCIS, 2017; RSPH, 2017; see, in online bibliography: House of Commons, 2019b; UK CMOs, 2019; ICO, 2019; Sam Levin, Facebook Told Advertisers It Can Identify When Teens Feeling 'Insecure' and 'Worthless', *Guardian*, 1 May 2017, www.theguardian.com/technology/2017/ may/01/facebook-advertising-data-insecure-teens. See also Livingstone, 2018: The LSE-Led Research Study on Children's Data and Privacy online is at www.lse.ac.uk/media-and-communications/research/research-projects/ childprivacyonline; Kurt Wagner, What Happens When You Get Off Facebook for Four Weeks? Stanford researchers found out, *Recode*, 27 February 2019, www.recode.net/2019/2/27/18243546/facebook-study-stanford-gentzkow-wellbeing-politcal-polarization; see, in online bibliography: Allcott et al., 2019; other studies include Baker and Algorta, 2016; Shane-Simpson et al., 2018; Faelens, 2019; Macrynikola and Miranda, 2019.

37 Mark Zuckerberg, A Blueprint for Content Governance and Enforcement, 15 November 2018 www.facebook.com/notes/mark-zuckerberg/a-blueprint-for-content-governance-and-enforcement/10156443129621634/; Alice Marwick and Rebecca Lewis, Media Manipulation and Disinformation Online, Data and Society, 15 May 2017, https://datasociety.net/output/media-manip-ulation-and-disinfo-online/; Whitney Phillips, The Oxygen of Amplification, Data and Society Research Institute, 22 May 2018, https://datasociety.net/out-put/oxygen-of-amplification/. Nicholas Thomson and Fred Vogelstein, Inside the Two Years That Shook Facebook and the World, *Wired*, 18 February 2018, www.wired.com/story/inside-facebook-mark-zuckerberg-2-years-of-hell/.

38 Josh Constine, Facebook Will Change Algorithm to Demote 'Borderline Content': That Almost Violates Policies, *Techcrunch*, 15 November 2018, https://techcrunch.com/2018/11/15/facebook-borderline-content/.

39 Renee DiResta, Online conspiracy Groups Are a Lot Like Cults, *Wired*, 13 November 2018, www.wired.com/story/online-conspiracy-groups-qanon-cults/; Sunstein, 2017.

40 Paul Lewis, 'Fiction Is Outperforming Reality': How YouTube's Algorithm Distorts Truth, *Guardian*, 2 February 2018, www.theguardian.com/technology/2018/feb/02/how-youtubes-algorithm-distorts-truth; Paul Lewis and Eric McCormick, How an Ex-YouTube Insider Investigated Its Secret Algorithm, *Guardian*, 2 February 2018, www.theguardian.com/technology/2018/feb/02/youtube-algorithm-election-clinton-trump-guillaume-chaslot; Zeynep Tufecki, YouTube the Great Radicalizer, *New York Times*, 10 March 2018, www.nytimes.com/2018/03/10/opinion/sunday/youtube-politics-radical.html; Rebecca Lewis, Alternative Influence: Broadcasting the Reactionary Right on YouTube, *Data and Society*, 18 September 2018, https://datasociety.net/output/alternative-influence/; Craig Silverman, Jane Lytvynenko, and Tham Puy Lo, How Facebook Groups Are Being Exploited to Spread Misinformation, Plan Harassment and Radicalize People, *Buzzfeed*, 19 March 2018, www.buzzfeednews.com/article/craigsilverman/how-facebook-groups-are-being-exploited-to-spread.

41 John Naughton, From self-Harm to Terrorism, Online Recommendations Cast a Deadly Shadow, *Observer* New Review, 3 March 2019, 23; Ysabel Gerrard and Tarleton Gillespie, When Algorithms Think You Want to Die, *Wired*, 21 February 2019, www.wired.com/story/when-algorithms-think-you-want-to-die/; Mark Bridge, Instagram Steers Teens to Harmful Images in Seconds, *The Times*, 2 February 2019, 17; Sarah Marsh, Instagram Urged to Act Over Anorexia Images, *Guardian*, 9 February 2019, 19.

5 Facebook and the media

> Our goal is to build the perfect personalized newspaper for every person in the world.
>
> – Mark Zuckerberg, 2014[1]

Facebook has disrupted the global media ecosystem. This chapter assesses the dependency relationship which Facebook's dominance has imposed upon the media sector as a whole; the question of whether Facebook itself is a media company and the implications which that has for debates on media plurality and diversity; the economics of online advertising; the 'fake news' distraction and the role of Facebook's News Feed; the decline of trust in established media and the rise of especially 'alt-right' news sites, which has been fuelled by Facebook.

The dependency relationship

The UK's Cairncross review examined how to create a sustainable future for journalism. There was a need to reset the 'unbalanced' relationship between news media organisations and news aggregating platforms, with new codes of conduct overseen by a regulator. Cairncross particularly notes the decline of UK newspapers: 'Print circulation has halved over the last ten years – national papers from 11.5m daily copies in 2008 to 5.8m in 2018 and for local papers from 63.4m weekly in 2007 to 31.4m weekly in 2017'.

These conclusions are borne out by academic research and industry surveys. Rasmus Kleis Nielsen and Susan Ganter argued that relationships between media organisations and social media platforms are characterised by 'a fear of missing out', by the difficulties of making a realistic assessment of the risks and opportunities of new platform initiatives and by 'asymmetry' in the relationship. News media are now increasingly in a dependent relationship with platforms, which hold structural power and act on the basis of their own interests.

Emily Bell and Taylor Owen showed that platforms not only act as distribution channels but 'control what audiences see' and even what kind of journalism flourishes. News organisations are losing out to platforms through 'loss of branding, the lack of audience data, and the migration of advertising revenue'. The structure and economics of platforms incentivises low-quality clickbait over high-quality material, emphasising share and scalability over investigative or minority journalism.[2]

Media organisations pump out more and more material, in different formats, on a variety of platforms, including Facebook's Instant Articles, designed to ensure fast-loading of news stories within the Facebook app (with the downside that traffic does not go to their websites), Live Video and Instagram Stories. There is an impact on news media branding: research shows that users are less likely to notice news sources if they receive the material via social media. 'I saw it on Facebook' has become something akin to folklore. Until recently, there was no branding difference in the Facebook News Feed between fake news sites and established and respected news outlets: all were formatted in Facebook's own style.[3]

Media organisations had to press Facebook for a year to get their branding included within Instant Articles. This is not to say that publishers have not received revenues: it's estimated that publishers received $3 billion from Facebook in 2016. But by 2018, the Colombia Journalism Review suggested that more than half of publishers who originally signed up for Instant Articles were no longer using it.

Harvard scholar Greg Piechota says, 'Facebook outperforms publishers in all major activities that previously created or captured value in the industry – from aggregation to distribution and advertising sales'. Piechota surveyed 37 news executives from US and European media brands about their relationship with Facebook. He found that Facebook helped increase reach and engagement but was not as open as they would like on product or algorithm changes – and advertising revenue returns were not sufficient. Facebook was felt to privilege some media partners above others.[4]

Premium-brand publishers are in a stronger position. I asked *New York Times* (*NYT*) chief executive Mark Thompson about their Facebook relationship at the 2019 Oxford Media Convention in open session. He said that it was 'complicated and interesting'. Facebook could be useful for getting the message out and as a marketing channel for subscriptions. The *NYT* will also advertise on Facebook to encourage those who see their content to become subscribers. But they limit the number of stories that they make available on Facebook.[5]

The economic model for news journalism was eroded as newspapers became unbundled, with Craigslist grabbing classified advertising and Google display, and the vertical integration of media organisations as revenue-raising distribution engines was disrupted.[6]

Media companies are dependent on changes to Facebook's News Feed. In late 2013, Facebook began to serve ads inviting users to like media pages, which caused a massive increase in traffic to media companies. But subsequent changes to the News Feed algorithm had a significant impact on traffic on particular digital news sites, when Facebook made algorithm changes to balance 'content from Friends and Pages' and reduce clickbait. Further changes to the News Feed in January 2018 have pushed up angry reactions and news on divisive topics.[7]

In 2015, Facebook adjusted the algorithm to give video higher visibility. This 'pivot to video' led to many publishers laying off journalists and investing instead in video production. Facebook had regular issues with its video metrics, which it acknowledged, but in the autumn of 2018, the *Wall Street Journal* revealed that publishers were now claiming in a California court case that these metrics were fraudulently, not accidentally, exaggerated by Facebook.[8]

The Cairncross Review cites research by Dr Rachel Howells in respect of the loss of the *Port Talbot Guardian* in South West Wales and the impact that this has had on local democracy. I saw similar issues in my former constituency of the Rhondda in the South Wales Valleys. When I was elected to the National Assembly for Wales in 2003, media research suggested that 60% of local people read the *Rhondda Leader*, which had a cover price of 32 pence, its own editor and dedicated local reporters working from an office in Pontypridd. By 2016, the newspaper price was over 90 pence, the editorial team had long been merged with other reporters, the local office was closed, local news content specifically from the Rhondda had significantly reduced and copy was often shared with other valleys' newspapers. NiemanLab has found the same phenomenon in the United States. Newspaper circulation in the United States has halved since the mid-1980s, and print newspaper advertising has fallen from $67 billion in 2000 to below $20 billion today, with US newspapers cutting 45% of their employees between 2008 and 2017; regional and local newspaper circulation has halved in Britain over the last decade, with a net loss of 245 titles.[9]

Is Facebook a media company?

Media organisations, and many academics, have argued that Facebook should be regarded as a media company or a publisher. Facebook has resisted such a definition, even though when announcing changes to the Facebook News Feed in 2013, Mark Zuckerberg said 'What we're trying to do is give everyone in the world the best personalised newspaper we can'. More surprisingly, seeking to resist the California court case brought by the app-maker Six4Three, Facebook lawyers said that the right to deny data to Six4Three and other developers was 'a quintessential publisher function' comparing this to the right of a newspaper. Yet Facebook continued to claim publicly that it was a technology company, not a media company.[10]

As Facebook announced that it was entering the market for original and licensed video content in December 2016, with Facebook Watch joining Facebook Live as an opening for media content, Mark Zuckerberg said that

> Facebook is a new kind of platform. It's not a traditional technology company. It's not a traditional media company.

In January 2017, Facebook announced its journalism project, a new programme 'to establish stronger ties between Facebook and the news industry', with three main elements: new collaborative tools for news journalism; training and tools for journalists; and training and tools for everyone else. Facebook now also shows major sports in the US and oversees.[11]

On a definitional basis, some argue that media companies create, post, curate, distribute and monetise content, although in the UK, Channel Four, for example, has operated on a publisher-broadcaster model of publishing content produced by others. Facebook's algorithm curates content, and it produces edited videos of users' activity for them to post to their pages. Natali Helberger has argued that we should consider Facebook as a 'social editor': the design choices of the Facebook algorithm shapes how users consume news. Facebook's famous censorship of the naked young Vietnamese girl fleeing Napalm, which became the subject of a row with the editor of the Norwegian newspaper *Aftenposten* and the Norwegian prime minister, its regular censorship of breast-feeding photographs, breast cancer awareness programmes, naked statues and many other examples, as well as deliberate actions to remove material offensive to governments around the world are all examples of an editorial role being played. Gillespie says that the switch from a chronological news feed to an algorithmically curated one meant that Facebook had started to produce 'a media commodity'.[12]

The Australian Competition and Consumer Commission (ACCC) has said platforms like Facebook 'increasingly perform similar functions as news media businesses such as selecting, publishing and ranking content, including significant amounts of news media content'. Academics and policy advocates have argued that platforms like Facebook need to be incorporated into sector-specific legislation on media plurality and diversity, designed to support a healthy public sphere with diverse media sources, content and exposure.[13] Facebook may be a publisher or a media company, but it is also an advertising platform, and analysing its role in the advertising market is key to addressing issues of market power.

The economics of online advertising

Current estimates are that the Facebook and Google duopoly account for a higher proportion of digital advertising revenue in the UK than in the US. Facebook's share was estimated at 22.7% in the UK in 2018 and Instagram's 4.9%. Facebook is forecast to grow to 28% by 2021 and Instagram to 9.4%. Google is forecast to decline from 40% in 2018 to 36.7% in 2021.[14]

Concentration of online and especially mobile advertising on two particularly dominant players such as Facebook and Google limits funding diversity with all its implications for source, content and exposure diversity, and the advertising industry has been at the forefront of recent criticisms of digital platforms. In the UK, a series of reports have now called for a Competition and Markets authority investigation into duopoly dominance of online advertising.[15]

In Australia, a market inquiry has already been undertaken on some of these issues. The Australian Competition and Consumer Commission (ACCC) found that both Facebook and Google had 'substantial market power' in certain markets. Sixty-eight per cent of advertising spend is going to the duopoly. The ACCC has said that they need particular scrutiny, because they are vertically integrated, that is, present at multiple levels of the same supply chain. Facebook is vertically integrated through the Facebook audience network and the services offered on Facebook platforms. The European Commission fined Google $1.7 billion for competition breaches in respect of its online advertising operation in March 2019.

The ACCC has found that there is a lack of transparency which means that 'advertisers do not know what they are paying for, where their advertisements are being displayed, and to whom'. As different regulatory conditions apply to digital platforms from media companies, the ACCC says there is a 'regulatory imbalance' which may provide an unfair advantage to platforms 'in attracting advertising expenditure.' The ACCC said there may be merit in a regulator monitoring the digital advertising market in respect of the behaviours of dominant players and the pricing of digital advertising.[16] Meanwhile, a US FTC Commissioner has also suggested that behavioural advertising technologies 'radically alter the relationship between platform, user, and content'. The German Cartel Authority has of course called Facebook's entire advertising model into question, unless it gets direct consent from users.[17]

Researchers Vian Bakir and Andrew McStay have called the modern fake news phenomenon an issue of the 'economics of emotion'. They suggest that the solution lies in part with the advertising industry and its potential to discipline the platforms. There has been a fightback against what *New York Times* chief executive Mark Thompson called the 'nightmarish joke' of the digital advertising market, with Proctor and Gamble and Unilever, the two largest global advertisers, in the lead. Proctor and Gamble slashed $200 million from its digital advertising budget without seeing any negative impact on its bottom line. Unilever said it would move money from sites that could not prove that the ads were being seen by humans rather than robots. Media stories in 2017 demonstrated that reputable companies were advertising, without knowing it, next to terrorist, hate-speech, criminal or pornographic content.[18]

The 'fake news' distraction

Facebook's role in news distribution rode to the top of the political agenda in many countries, following the 2016 UK Brexit referendum outcome and the election of Donald Trump in the US.[19] Buzzfeed's Craig Silverman reported that fake news stories – such as the idea that the pope had endorsed Trump – recorded more engagements on Facebook than did real news items in the period from August to November 2016. Silverman and his colleague Lawrence Alexander also found fake news factories in a variety of places, perhaps most surprisingly, the town of Veles in Macedonia, where teenagers were reported to be earning good incomes from manufacturing items set to appeal to Trump supporters. Fake news 'factories' were also recorded closer to home. Within weeks of his election, President Trump had appropriated the words to use against media outlets with which he disagreed.

Media scholar Dr Claire Wardle sought definitional clarity over the term *fake news*, which she called 'a woefully inadequate phrase'. Her work has been influential in policy terms, particularly at a European level. She and others successfully expanded the discussion from a narrow focus on 'fake news' to a conceptually richer examination of misinformation, disinformation and what she and Hossein Derakhshan have called mal-information. Meanwhile, the EU's high-level group (EC, 2018) has produced a series of recommendations which offer proposals for countering fake news and disinformation without introducing content censorship. The group favoured use of the term *disinformation* to cover all kinds of false, inaccurate or misleading information and urged multi-stakeholder collaboration to address the problems, based on a Code of Practices reflecting the varying responsibilities of different stakeholders, with public authorities taking an enabling role.[20]

Immediately after the US election, the respected digital sociologist Zeynep Tufekci tweeted that Facebook's News Feed algorithm had been central to its outcome. Tufekci had been an early critic of the algorithmic sorting of Facebook's News Feed and challenged the company's own research which sought to dispel the notion that it created a filter bubble. She had demonstrated that the News Feed had diminished coverage of the shooting by Ferguson, Missouri, police of an African-American male, Michael Brown, in August 2014 and the protests that took place following this, while elevating coverage of the ice-bucket charity challenge. As she said, the News Feed algorithm is 'dynamic, all but invisible, and individually tailored'.[21]

There are clear economic incentives for purveyors of fake news and disinformation: more likes, more shares and more clicks lead to more money for Facebook pages and Facebook as a platform. As one former Facebook product manager posted in November 2016,

> Sadly, News Feed optimizes for engagement. As we've learned in this election, bullshit is highly engaging.

Users who are made angry or anxious by particular posts are more likely to share such items, particularly if they are members of networks driven by particular partisan beliefs, such as conspiracy theorists. Extensive research by Cambridge University in the UK recently identified the prevalence of a range of conspiracy theories where significant numbers believed the authorities were keeping facts from them. These included doubts about immigration figures, belief in a Muslim plot to take over, anti-vaccination theories and hostility to global warming.[22]

Survey evidence has suggested that most Facebook users are unaware that an algorithm does the sorting of their News Feed. For a significant period after 2016, the key questions were whether Facebook's News Feed acted, as Pariser has suggested, as a filter bubble or, as Sunstein has argued, allowed the easier formulation of echo chambers. Stereotypical 'conservative' and 'liberal' News Feeds were rigged up to demonstrate the potentially divisive nature of the distribution effects.[23]

Academic commentators started to unpick some of the reasoning behind the claims that Facebook's News Feed could have dictated the outcome of the result, pointing to decades of research on media campaign and persuasion effects and influence in psychology, media studies and political science. People often receive their news mediated by social context (e.g., the sharing by community or national opinion-formers, which post-war research by Katz and Lazarsfeld termed the 'two-step' flow of communication). Therefore, the assumption that individuals cast their votes because of the nature of the news they consumed through their Facebook News Feed was overly simplistic. There is significant research evidence to suggest that people, including heavy Facebook users, are not insulated from other perspectives, and that their media diets include news likely to challenge their political attitudes; that pre-existing views profoundly shape people's beliefs, as we have a tendency to confirmation bias, or homophily; and that people with different political views will derive different meanings from news presented to them: their receptivity is grounded in attitudinal and contextual ways. Additionally, while fake news was widely read and shared, the extent that individual US citizens were exposed to fake news should not be over-estimated, television news was a more significant source, the news selections of print and broadcast journalism gave more attention to Hillary Clinton's emails than her policies and so on. Other research showed that the bulk of visits to and sharing of 'fake news' items came from a very small section of the overall electorate and that partisan identification played an important role in this.[24]

Social media organisations like Facebook present political news and opinion in the News Feed in the context of a flow of personal news and engagement, gossip, sport and celebrity commentary, which means users may encounter views that they would otherwise avoid. Understanding the difference between exposure to news and consumption of such information is important, with social media's interactivity and engagement by users providing one element of that understanding. Sharing of news items by friends and family members trumps selection by partisan identification. Martin Moore says that by leveraging the power of friends, Facebook enables the hacking of Katz and Lazarsfeld's two-step flow. What happens, says Alice Marwick in an important recent article, is that 'virtually every story is augmented with someone's opinion'. She says that scholars and journalists are only just 'beginning to understand the myriad impacts of social sharing'. In seeking to develop a 'sociotechnical' model of media effects, she says, 'fake news' must be understood as part of 'a larger media ecosystem'. It is not simply a problem of pre-existing polarisation, of online advertising or algorithmic sorting, of a more sustained extreme right politics or right-tilting media environment: all of these things matter.[25]

Attention has increasingly switched to the closely integrated alt-right news network, which includes a wide variety of online publications and news stations, websites and Facebook groups and advertising identified shortly after the 2016 election by Dr Jonathan Albright. Albright demonstrated that while Facebook certainly performed an amplifying and enraging function, the real issue was the sourcing of the original output from within the highly integrated alt-right media ecosystem of real-time propaganda. Research by Jose van Dijck and others shows that Facebook 'substantially contributed to the development of an insulated right-wing media system'. The most substantial research on the subject says that the fundamental

explanation cannot be blamed on Facebook, new technology or indeed Russian propaganda. While these are important, there is a danger, argue Yochai
Benkler and others, in short-term approaches, which could fail to address
long-term trends. Their data support the claim of President Trump's campaign manager, Steve Bannon, that 'Facebook is what propelled Breitbart
to a massive audience'. But Facebook's was the primary source of news for
only 7% of Donald Trump voters, compared with Fox News which was the
primary source for 40% of them.[26]

Mark Zuckerberg initially responded after the US election that the idea
that Facebook had caused the election outcome was 'a pretty crazy idea'.
Within a week of the election, he had announced a series of initiatives that
Facebook was going to take to address the problem of 'misinformation',
including reducing incentives to share fake news and introducing fact-
checking, and by September 2017, he was apologising for his initial reaction. By early 2019, however, a number of fact-checking organisations, such
as Snopes, had given up on helping Facebook. Around the world, Facebook
was working with 43 fact-checking organisations in 24 different languages –
but at the beginning of 2019, it imposed a monthly payment cap, typically
40 articles per month per agency. But Facebook also moved to downgrade
the News Feed impact of groups that repeatedly shared misinformation.[27]

Facebook has of course been on the defensive about the News Feed since
2016 when Gizmodo suggested that human moderators were reducing the
quantity of US conservative news seen. Mark Zuckerberg allegedly had to
re-assure conservative politicians and publishers that there would be no bias
against them, and human monitoring was reduced. Indeed, staff who performed an editorial curation role left the company in 2016 and subsequently
had a few choice things to say about the 'fake news' scandal after the US
presidential election. Trending Topics was closed down in 2018.[28]

One of Mark Zuckerberg's solutions when the News Feed algorithm was
changed again in January 2018 was to suggest that trusted sources could be
elevated in the News Feed and that views of what outlets should be trusted
could be out-sourced to Facebook users. Zuckerberg said,

> The hard question we've struggled with is how to decide what news
> sources are broadly trusted in a world with so much division. We could
> try to make that decision ourselves, but that's not something we're
> comfortable with. . . . We decided that having the community determine
> which sources are broadly trusted would be most objective.[29]

Yet surveys in the US indicate strong partisan alignment in respect of trust
in established media organisations and indeed social media. Trust in mainstream media institutions from organisations on the right of politics has

diminished particularly in the United States following the ending of the Fairness doctrine in the 1980s, the growth of shock-jocks and the launch of Fox News. Measurement of trust in the media and journalism generally, as distinct from specific news organisations such as (say) the BBC or the *New York Times*, often produces highly negative results. Trust in the media was measured across 37 countries by the Reuter's Institute (2018), showing variable degrees of media trust in different countries, but there was a tendency for people to trust the media that they themselves used. The decline in trust pre-dates Facebook. Gallup records trust in journalism as having plunged from 72% in 1976 to 32% in 2016 – and only 14% among Republicans. Perhaps encouragingly there has been a recovery from that low point, although trust among Republicans remains at only 21%.[30]

While some have called for Facebook to undertake proper editorial curation, creating a hierarchy of trusted news outlets, others worry about the power that this gives Facebook. Trust in media, as we have seen, is contextual, influenced by personal preference and experience and social and historical events.

Funding quality journalism

One of the recommendations of the Cairncross Review is that ways should be found to ensure greater prominence for quality news. Some major newspaper brands have been able to generate subscriber and membership income at a meaningful level and have been able to leverage their brands for advertising revenue. Facebook's Journalism Project has committed to spending $300 million to help local newsrooms in local papers around the United States and local journalists in other countries, spending for example £4.5 million on 80 local journalists in the UK. However, Facebook said in March 2019 that 40% of people in the United States lived in areas where there were no local newspapers at all, making it impossible to support local journalism in those areas.[31]

There have been calls for Facebook to support quality journalism through the payment of 'carriage fees'. Media organisations have argued for some time that Facebook – and Google – is developing its social network by raising advertising revenues against media content circulated sometimes illegally by users, and they should be compensated for this. In 2019, the European Union adopted a new Copyright Directive opposed by the Big Tech companies. One response to this by Facebook, dressed in the guise of supporting journalism, has been to suggest that its role in this might be to build a dedicated section of its website for 'trusted' news. Since Facebook will have to compensate publishers under the Copyright Directive in two years' time, this could simply be a reactive move. Other moves under consideration by lawmakers and regulators include varying anti-trust law, allowing news organisations to negotiate collectively with platforms, and a recent suggestion that platforms should lose their Section 230 protection under the 1996 Communications Decency Act, one of the foundations of US regulation in the Internet era, since they are no longer passive conveyors of user-generated content but are instead actively soliciting, algorithmically sorting and repurposing content.[32]

Cairncross suggested direct funding including innovation funding for public-interest news and tax reliefs for publishers for online news and local and investigative news. Some countries of course have newspaper subsidies in place. Meanwhile, a variety of organisations have suggested a levy on online platform profits to support quality journalism. Meanwhile, Facebook provides its own subsidies through sponsored content relationships with news media organisations to promote its arguments and downplay criticisms.[33]

Notes

1 Widely quoted, for example Eugene Kim, Mark Zuckerberg Wants to Build 'the Perfect Personalized Newspaper' for Every Person in the World, *Business Insider*, 6 November 2014, www.businessinsider.com/mark-zuckerberg-wants-to-build-a-perfect-personalized-newspaper-2014-11?r=US&IR=T.
2 Cairncross, 2019; Nielsen and Ganter, 2018. Other studies illustrate these issues of dependency: Nielsen, 2018; Emily Bell and Taylor Owen, The Platform Press; How Silicon Valley Re-Engineered Journalism, *Tow Center*, 29 March 2017, www.cjr.org/tow_center_reports/platform-press-how-silicon-valley-reeng ineered-journalism.php; John Lanchester, You Are the Product, *London Review of Books*, 17 August 2017, www.lrb.co.uk/v39/n16/john-lanchester/ you-are-the-product; Jamie Condliffe, Fake News Is Unbelievably Cheap to Produce, *MIT Technology Review*, 14 June 2017, www.technologyreview. com/s/608105/fake-news-is-unbelievably-cheap/; Mathew Ingram, The Facebook Armageddon, *Columbia Journalism Review*, Winter 2018, www.cjr.org/ special_report/facebook-media-buzzfeed.php/; Facebook's role in driving traffic to media sites has fluctuated with changes in its algorithm: Conrad Lee, Facebook Declines, Google Grows as Battle for News Audiences Continues, *Parse.ly*, 30 November 2017, https://blog.parse.ly/post/6663/facebook-declines-google-grows-news-audiences/.
3 Amy Mitchell Elisa Shearer, Jeffrey Gottfried Kristine Lu, How Americans Encounter, Recall and Act Upon Digital News, *Pew Research Center*, 9 February 2017, www.journalism.org/2017/02/09/how-americans-encounter-recall-and-act-upon-digital-news/; Mark Sweney, Facebook's Rise as News Source Hits Publisher Revenues, *Guardian*, 15 June 2016, www.theguardian.com/ media/2016/jun/15/facebooks-news-publishers-reuters-institute-for-the-study-of-journalism; Alex Hern, Here's How Facebook Can Tackle Fake News, *Guardian*, 26 November 2016, www.theguardian.com/technology/2016/nov/25/

facebook-fake-news-fight-mark-zuckerberg; Pew Research Institute, 2016; Dr Antonis Kalogeropoulos and Nic Newman, I saw the news on Facebook, Reuter's Institute for the Study of Journalism, nd 2017, https://reutersinstitute. politics.ox.ac.uk/our-research/i-saw-news-facebook-brand-attribution-when-accessing-news-distributed-environments.

4 Instant Articles, Facebook, https://instantarticles.fb.com; Nielsen, 2018; Pete Brown, More Than Half of Facebook Instant Articles Partners May Have Abandoned It, *Columbia Journalism Review*, 2 February 2018, www.cjr.org/ tow_center/are-facebook-instant-articles-worth-it.php?utm_source=Trigger mail&utm_medium=email&utm_campaign=Post%20Blast%20%28bii-digital-media%29:%20Publishers%20turn%20away%20from%20Facebook%20Instant %20Articles%20-%20Apple%20Music%20inches%20closer%20to%20rival%20 Spotify%20-%20Netflix%20faces%20uphill%20battle%20in%20India&utm_ term=BII%20List%20DMedia%20ALL; Greg Piechota, The Facebook-Media Relationship: It's Complicated, International News Media Association, 27 September 2016, www.inma.org/report-detail.cfm?pubid=189.

5 Author's notes, Oxford Media Convention, 18 March 2019.

6 Since Facebook is essentially hosting, distributing and monetizing, it is also gathering more and more lucrative user data. Ben Thompson, The Great Unbundling, *Stratechery*, 18 January 2017, https://stratechery.com/2017/the-great-unbundling/; Turow, 2012; Facebook has significant market power after buying Crowdtangle, the service which helps publishers evaluate which content was getting most engagement: Casey Newton, Facebook Buys Crowdtangle, the Tool Publishers Use to Win the Internet, *The Verge*, 11 November 2016, www. theverge.com/2016/11/11/13594338/facebook-acquires-crowdtangle, and Atlas, the advertising measurement service: Brian Boland, Facebook to Acquire Atlas from Microsoft, *Facebook Newsroom*, 28 February 2013, https://newsroom.fb. com/news/2013/02/facebook-to-acquire-atlas-from-microsoft/and Christl and Spiekermann, 2016.

7 On Facebook inviting users to like media pages, see Alexis C. Madrigal, What Facebook Did to American Democracy, *The Atlantic*, 12 October 2017, www.theatlantic.com/technology/archive/2017/10/what-facebook-did/542502/; Max Eulenstein and Lauren Scissors, Balancing Content from Friends and Pages, *Facebook Newsroom*, 21 April 2015, https://news room.fb.com/news/2015/04/news-feed-fyi-balancing-content-from-friends-and-pages/; Mark Zuckerberg, *Facebook*, 12 January 2018, www.facebook. com/search/top/?q=zuckerberg%20time%20well%20spent&epa=SEARCH_ BOX; Laura Hazard Owen, One Year in, Facebook's Big Algorithm Change Has Spurred an Angry, Fox News Dominated, and Very Engaged News Feed, *NiemanLab*, 15 March 2019, www.niemanlab.org/2019/03/one-year-in-face books-big-algorithm-change-has-spurred-an-angry-fox-news-dominated-and-very-engaged-news-feed/, based on Newswhip, 2019 Guide to Facebook Publishing, http://go.newswhip.com/2019_03-FacebookPublishing_LP.html; Guy Rosen and Tessa Lyons, Remove, Reduce, Inform: New Steps to Manage Problematic Content, *Facebook Newsroom*, 10 April 2019, https://newsroom. fb.com/news/2019/04/remove-reduce-inform-new-steps/?utm_campaign= The%20Interface&utm_medium=email&utm_source=Revue%20newsletter; even digital publishers haven't been immune to Facebook's impact: Keach Hagey and Lukas I. Alpert, Vice, Buzzfeed and the Reckoning for New-Media Companies, *Wall Street Journal*, 1 February 2019, www.wsj.com/articles/vice-media-

cuts-250-jobs-or-10-of-workforce-11549033923: Emily Bell, What 2000 Job Cuts Tell Us: The Free Market Kills Digital Journalism, *Guardian*, 2 February 2019, www.theguardian.com/media/2019/feb/02/what-2000-job-cuts-tell-us-the-free-market-kills-digital-journalism.

8 For an overview of Facebook's strategic shift to video, see Laura Hazard Owen, Did Facebook's Faulty Data Push News Publishers to Make Terrible Decisions on Video? *NiemanLab*, 17 October 2017, www.niemanlab.org/2018/10/did-facebooks-faulty-data-push-news-publishers-to-make-terrible-decisions-on-video/; David Fischer, An Update on Facebook Video Metrics, 23 September 2016, www.facebook.com/business/news/facebook-video-metrics-update?mod=article_inline: for the California court documents, see www.documentcloud.org/documents/5004295-d5cb8373-8cbb-4e81-9710-f2ccf44 81b74.html; Danny Fortson and Simon Duke, Zuckerberg's Missing Millions on Facebook, *Sunday Times*, 28 January 2018, www.thetimes.co.uk/article/zuckerbergs-missing-millions-on-facebook-7tpqvg2c9.

9 Rachel Howells, *Journey to the Centre of a News Black Hole: Examining the Democratic Deficit in a Town with No Newspaper*, PhD Thesis, June 2015, 59, http://orca.cf.ac.uk/87313/1/2016howellsrphd.pdf (see also Baldwin, 2018; Moore, 2018); on the Rhondda, see James Thomas, John Jewell and Stephen Cushion, Media Coverage of the 2003 Welsh Assembly Election, Wales Media Forum, Centre for Journalism Studies, Cardiff University, 2003; Joshua Benton, When Local Newspapers Shrink, Fewer People Bother to Run for Mayor, *NiemanLab*, 9 April 2019, www.niemanlab.org/2019/04/when-local-newspapers-shrink-fewer-people-bother-to-run-for-mayor/; Margaret Sullivan, Most People Think Local Journalism Is Financially Healthy: Here's the Troubling Reality, *Washington Post*, 31 March 2019, www.washingtonpost.com/lifestyle/style/most-people-think-local-journalism-is-financially-healthy-heres-the-troubling-reality/2019/03/31/c77e4790-5227-11e9-a3f7-78b7525a8d5f_story.html?utm_term=.262a5e609bb7; Freddy Mayhew, UK Local Newspaper Closures: Net Loss of 245 Titles Since 2005, New Press Gazette Research, *Press Gazette*, 11 February 2019, www.pressgazette.co.uk/more-than-40-local-news-titles-closed-in-2018-with-loss-of-some-editorial-275-jobs-new-figures-show/.

10 Stewart Purvis, Showdown Looms for the Net Giants, *Television*, Royal Television Society, May 2017, 14–15; Jim Edwards, Here's what Mark Zuckerberg Thinks a Newspaper Should Look Like, *Business Insider*, 7 March 2013, www.businessinsider.com/heres-what-mark-zuckerberg-thinks-a-newspaper-should-look-like-2013-3?r=US&IR=T; Eugene Kim, supra note 1. Facebook as personalized newspaper was stressed in induction sessions for new employees by senior Facebook executive Chris Cox (Martinez, 2016: 260–261); Sam Levin, Is Facebook a Publisher? In Public It Says No, But in Court It Says Yes, *Guardian*, 3 July 2018, www.theguardian.com/technology/2018/jul/02/facebook-mark-zuckerberg-platform-publisher-lawsuit; Giulia Segreti, Facebook CEO Says Group Will Not Become a Media Company, *Reuters*, 29 August 2016, www.reuters.com/article/us-facebook-zuckerberg-idUSKCN1141WN.

11 Dave Lee, Another Big Sports Deal for Facebook, *BBC News Online*, 14 August 2018, www.bbc.co.uk/news/technology-45178848.

12 On Facebook Live, see Pippa Shawley, A Fresh Face for Storytelling, *Television*, Royal Television Society, October 2016, 46–47 and on video expansion, Hannah Kuchler and Shannon Bond, Facebook Has Its Eyes on the Next Video Prize, *Financial Times*, 17–18 June 2012, 15; Samuel Gibbs, Mark Zuckerberg

Appears to Finally Admit Facebook Is a Media Company, *Guardian*, 22 December 2016, www.theguardian.com/technology/2016/dec/22/mark-zuckerberg-appears-to-finally-admit-facebook-is-a-media-company; Fidji Simo, Introducing: The Facebook Journalism Project, *Facebook Newsroom*, 11 January 2017, www.facebook.com/facebookmedia/blog/introducing-the-facebook-journalism-project; on Facebook Watch, see Nick Grudin, Introducing Watch and Shows on Facebook, Facebook for Media, 9 August 2017, www.facebook.com/facebookmedia/blog/introducing-watch-and-shows-on-facebook. On the question of whether Facebook should be subject to TV-like audience measures, see Should Facebook and Google Join in? *Television*, October 2018, 23; Amol Rajan, Facebook: Social Network, Media Company, or Both? *BBC News Online*, 15 December 2016, www.bbc.co.uk/news/entertainment-arts-38333249; Alice Ross and Julie Carrie Wong, Facebook Deletes Norwegian PM's Post as 'Napalm Girl' Row Escalates, *Guardian*, 9 September 2016, www.theguardian.com/technology/2016/sep/09/facebook-deletes-norway-pms-post-napalm-girl-post-row; Helberger, 2016; Gillespie, 2018: 43; Facebook's emphasis on monetisation is not counter-balanced by professional editorial ethics: Tufekci, 2015; Kreiss and McGregor, 2018.

13 Foster, 2012; Napoli and Caplan, 2017.

14 Facebook and Google Control Ever-Greater Portion of UK Ad Market, *e-Marketer*, 26 March 2019, www.emarketer.com/content/facebook-and-google-control-ever-greater-portion-of-uk-ad-market.

15 House of Commons, 2018a; House of Lords, 2018b; Furman, 2019; Cairncross, 2019, House of Commons, 2019b; House of Lords, 2019. The UK Chancellor of the Exchequer has now written to the CMA, Letter from the chancellor of the Exchequer to Lord Tyrie, Chairman of the CMA, 13 March 2019, https://assets.publishing.service.gov.uk/government/uploads/system/uploads/attachment_data/file/785552/Chancellor_letter_to_Lord_Tyrie_on_digital_advertising_130319.pdf; Letter from the CMA to Damian Collins M.P., 15 November 2018, http://data.parliament.uk/writtenevidence/committeeevidence.svc/evidencedocument/digital-culture-media-and-sport-committee/disinformation-and-fake-news/written/92618.html; Simon McDougall, Addressing the Adtech Debate from a Data Protection Perspective, *Information Commissioner's Office Blog*, n.d., https://ico.org.uk/about-the-ico/news-and-events/blog-advancing-the-adtech-debate-from-a-data-protection-perspective/.

16 Rod Sims, Examining the Impact of Digital Platforms on Competition in Media and Advertising Markets, 27 February 2019, www.accc.gov.au/speech/examining-the-impact-of-digital-platforms-on-competition-in-media-and-advertising-markets.

17 Prepared remarks of Federal Trade Commissioner Rohit Chopra, Tech platforms, Content Creators, and Immunity, 28 March 2019, www.ftc.gov/system/files/documents/public_statements/1510713/chopra_-_aba_spring_meeting_3-28-19.pdf; Emily Dreyfuss, German Regulators Just Outlawed Facebook's Entire Ad Business, *Wired*, 7 February 2019, www.wired.com/story/germany-facebook-antitrust-ruling/.

18 Personal notes, Oxford Media Convention, 2017; Bakir and McStay, 2018: 155; Brian Morrissey, The New York Times CEO on State of Digital Advertising: 'Nightmarish Joke', *Digiday*, 19 June 2017, https://digiday.com/media/new-york-times-ceo-state-digital-advertising-nightmarish-joke/; Siddharth Cavale, P&G Says It Cut $200m from Digital Ad Spend in 2017, *Reuters*, 1 March 2018,

https://uk.reuters.com/article/us-procter-gamble-advertising/pg-says-cut-digital-ad-spend-by-200-million-in-2017-idUKKCN1GD654; Iosifidis and Andrews, 2019; Craig Timberg, Elizabeth Dwoskin and Andrew Ba Tran, Mainstream Advertising Is Still Showing Up on Polarizing and Misleading Sites – Despite Efforts to Stop It, *Washington Post*, 3 October 2018, www.washingtonpost.com/business/technology/ads-from-mainstream-businesses-are-still-showing-up-on-extremist-sites--despite-efforts-to-stop-it/2018/10/03/6932974e-c326-11e8-8f06-009b39c3f6dd_story.html?utm_term=.3b342360863e; Simon Duke, Thousands of Jobs at Risk in WPP Overhaul, *The Times*, 8 December 2018, 54.

19 Katerina Eva Matsa and Elisa Shearer, News Use Across Social Media Platforms 2018, *Pew Research Center*, www.journalism.org/2018/09/10/news-use-across-social-media-platforms-2018/. *Post-truth* was the Oxford Dictionary's word of 2016: A range of books on post-truth and fake news was published, including in this series, McNair, 2018.

20 Wardle, 2018; Wardle and Derakhshan, 2017; EC, 2018.

21 Bakshy et al., 2015; Tufekci, 2015: 208.

22 See Bobby Goodlatte, *Facebook Post*, 9 November 2016, www.facebook.com/g/posts/10101648538367704?pnref=story; Farhad Manjoo, Can Facebook Fix Its Own Worst Bug? *New York Times* magazine, 25 April 2017, www.nytimes.com/2017/04/25/magazine/can-facebook-fix-its-own-worst-bug.html; Esther Addley, Study Shows 60% of Britons Believe in Conspiracy Theories, *Guardian*, 23 November 2018; www.theguardian.com/society/2018/nov/23/study-shows-60-of-britons-believe-in-conspiracy-theories; Hugo Drochon, Britons Are Swallowing Conspiracy Theories: Here's How to Stop the Rot, *Guardian*, 28 November 2018, www.theguardian.com/commentisfree/2018/nov/28/britons-swallowing-conspiracy-theories-stop-rot-research-fake-news; John Naughton, Populism and the Internet – a Toxic Mix Shaping the Age of Conspiracy Theories, *Observer*, 25 November 2018, www.theguardian.com/commentisfree/2018/nov/25/populism-and-the-internet-a-toxic-mix-shaping-the-age-of-conspiracy-theories; Facebook announced it would reduce the ranking of groups spreading disinformation about vaccination in March 2019.

23 On the ignorance of users about algorithmic sorting, see Foer, 2017: 73; on filter bubbles and echo chambers, Pariser, 2011; Sunstein, 2017. These terms have become useful but over-used heuristics. Jon Keegan, Blue Feed, Red Feed, *Wall Street Journal*, 18 May 2016, http://graphics.wsj.com/blue-feed-red-feed/#methodology; Julie Carrie Wong, Sam Levin and Olivia Solon, Bursting the Facebook Bubble: We Asked Voters on the Left and Right to Swap Feeds, *Guardian*, 16 November 2016, www.theguardian.com/us-news/2016/nov/16/facebook-bias-bubble-us-election-conservative-liberal-news-feed. Useful correctives of the determinist view that Facebook was responsible can be found at Keith Hampton and Esther Hargittai, Stop Blaming Facebook for Trump's Election Win, *The Hill*, 23 November 2016, https://thehill.com/blogs/pundits-blog/presidential-campaign/307438-stop-blaming-facebook-for-trumps-election-win; and Christian Vaccari, How Prevalent Are Filter Bubbles and Echo Chambers on Social Media? Not as Much as Conventional Wisdom Suggests, 14 March 2018, https://blog.lboro.ac.uk/crcc/uncategorised/prevalent-filter-bubbles-echo-chambers-social-media-not-much-conventional-wisdom/.

24 Katz et al., 1955. See online bibliography for up-to-date research on 'fake news', echo chambers and filter bubbles.

25 Toff and Nielsen, 2018; Moore, 2018: 125; Marwick, 2018.

26   Jonathan Albright, The #Election2016 Micro-Propaganda Machine, *Medium*, 18 November 2016, https://medium.com/@d1gi/the-election2016-micro-pro paganda-machine-383449cc1fba, and Data Is the Real Post-Truth, 28 November 2016, https://medium.com/@d1gi/data-is-the-real-post-truth-so-heres-the-truth-about-post-election2016-propaganda-2bff5ae1dd7; Issie Lapowsky, Shadow Politics: Meet the Digital Sleuth Exposing Fake News, *Wired*, 18 July 2018, www.wired.com/story/shadow-politics-meet-the-digital-sleuth-exposing-fake-news/; Van Dijck et al., 2018; Benkler et al., 2018. Baldwin (2018: 203) also identifies how changes to Facebook's algorithm from 2012–2013 helped the growth of Breitbart and other alt-right sites with their 'clickbait viral headlines'.

27   Olivia Solon, Facebook's Fake News: Mark Zuckerberg Rejects 'Crazy Idea' That It Could Have Swayed Voters, *Guardian*, 11 November 2016, www.theguardian.com/technology/2016/nov/10/facebook-fake-news-us-election-mark-zucker berg-donald-trump; Mark Zuckerberg, *Facebook Post*, 19 November 2016, www.facebook.com/zuck/posts/10103269806149061; Sam Levin, Mark Zuckerberg: I Regret Ridiculing Fears Over Facebook's Effect on Election, *Guardian*, 28 September 2017, www.theguardian.com/technology/2017/sep/27/mark-zuckerberg-facebook-2016-election-fake-news; Vinny Green and David Mikkelson, A Message to Our Community Regarding the Facebook Fact-Checking Partnership, *Snopes*, 1 February 2019, www.snopes.com/snopes-fb-partnership-ends/; Dave Lee, Matter of Fact-Checkers: Is Facebook Winning the Fake News War? *BBC News Online*, 2 April 2019, www.bbc.co.uk/news/technology-47779782; Jacob Kestrenakes, Facebook Will Punish Groups for Repeatedly Spreading Fake News, *The Verge*, 10 April 2019, www.theverge.com/2019/4/10/18304739/facebook-groups-reduce-misinformation-harmful-content-changes-messenger.

28   Michael Nunez, Former Facebook Workers: We Routinely Suppressed Conservative News, *Gizmodo*, 10 May 2016, https://gizmodo.com/former-facebook-workers-we-routinely-suppressed-conser-1775461006; Sarah Frier and Jennifer Jacobs, Zuckerberg Acknowledges Trust Gap After Meeting on Bias, *Bloomberg*, 19 May 2016, www.bloomberg.com/news/articles/2016-05-18/zuckerberg-acknowledges-trust-gap-after-meeting-on-facebook-bias; Tanya Dua, A Petri Dish of Bullshit, Confessions of Ex-Facebook News Curators, *Digiday*, 18 November 2016, https://digiday.com/media/petri-dish-bullshit-confessions-former-facebook-trending-news-curators/; Sarah Frier and Steven T. Dennis, Cruz Grills Zuckerberg on Censorship, Political Viewpoints, *Bloomberg*, 10 April 2018, www.bloomberg.com/news/articles/2018-04-10/cruz-grills-zucker berg-on-censorship-conservative-viewpoints; Alex Hardiman, Removing Trending from Facebook, *Facebook Newsroom*, 4 June 2018, https://newsroom.fb.com/news/2018/06/removing-trending/.

29   Adam Mosseri, Helping Ensure News on Facebook Is from Trusted Sources, *Facebook Newsroom*, 19 January 2018, https://newsroom.fb.com/news/2018/01/trusted-sources/.

30   Amy Mitchell, Jeffrey Gottfried, Michael Bartha and Nami Sumida, Distinguishing Between Factual and Opinion Statements in the News, *Pew Research Center*, 18 June 2018, www.journalism.org/2018/06/18/distinguishing-between-factual-and-opinion-statements-in-the-news/; Perceived Accuracy and Bias in the News Media, *Knight Foundation*, 20 June 2018, www.knightfoundation.org/reports/perceived-accuracy-and-bias-in-the-news-media; Jennifer Kavanagh and Michael D. Rich, Countering Truth Decay, *Rand Corporation*, 2018, www.

rand.org/research/projects/truth-decay.html; Nic Newman, Overview and Key Findings of the Digital News Report 2018, Reuter's Institute for the Study of Journalism, 30 May 2018, www.digitalnewsreport.org/survey/2018/overview-key-findings-2018/; On Gallup trust measures, see Andrew Edgecliffe-Johnson, I've Spent 20 Years Believing I Was Trusted to Report the News Objectively; Then I Went to Kentucky, *Financial Times Life and Arts*, 18–19 November 2017, 1 and Jeffrey M. Jones, US Media Trust Continues to Recover from 2016 Low, *Gallup*, 12 October 2018; Baldwin, 2018.

31 John Lanchester, You Are the Product, *London Review of Books*, 17 August 2017, www.lrb.co.uk/v39/n16/john-lanchester/you-are-the-product; Christine Schmidt, Facebook Is Committing $300 Million to Support News, with an Emphasis on Local, *NiemanLab*, 15 January 2019, www.niemanlab.org/2019/01/facebook-is-committing-300-million-to-support-news-with-an-emphasis-on-local/; Jim Waterson, Facebook Gives £4.5m to Fund 80 Local Newspaper Jobs in UK, www.theguardian.com/technology/2018/nov/19/facebook-gives-45m-to-fund-80-local-newspaper-jobs-in-uk-media: Associated Press, Facebook Local News Project Frustrated – by Lack of Local Newspapers, *Guardian*, 19 March 2019, www.theguardian.com/technology/2019/mar/18/facebook-local-news-project-frustrated-by-lack-of-local-newspapers.

32 Facebook should pay 'trusted' news publishers carriage fee: Murdoch, *Reuters*, 22 January 2018, https://uk.reuters.com/article/us-facebook-media-murdoch/facebook-should-pay-trusted-news-publishers-carriage-fee-murdoch-idUKKBN1FB2OG; Tom Knowles, Facebook May Pay for News Content, *The Times*, 3 April 2019, www.thetimes.co.uk/article/facebook-may-pay-for-news-content-bhbjwtdlx; Keach Hagey, Lawmakers Look to Even Playing Field Between News Media, Tech Titans, *Wall Street Journal*, 2 April 2019, www.wsj.com/articles/lawmakers-look-to-even-playing-field-between-news-media-tech-titans-11554238778; Chopra, supra n17.

33 Rob Price, Facebook Is Partnering with a Big UK Newspaper to Publish Sponsored Articles Downplaying 'Technofears' and Praising the Company, *Business Insider*, 3 April 2019, www.businessinsider.com/facebook-daily-telegraph-positive-sponsored-news-stories-2019-4?r=US&IR=T.

6 Facebook and democracy

> We hope to change how people relate to their governments and social institutions.
>
> – Mark Zuckerberg, 2012[1]

On November 16, 2010, FBI Director Robert Mueller burst into a meeting in Facebook's Silicon Valley headquarters to meet and shake hands with Mark Zuckerberg. Mueller was at Facebook because Zuckerberg had 'a better database' than the FBI did.[2]

The word *democracy* barely features in Mark Zuckerberg's notorious 5,737-word 2017 'manifesto'. Zuckerberg noted that

> In recent campaigns around the world – from India and Indonesia across Europe to the United States – we've seen the candidate with the largest and most engaged following on Facebook usually wins.[3]

Instead of democracy or democratisation, 'Facebook stands for bringing us closer together and building a global community.' *Connect* or *connection* are the most frequently used words to describe Facebook's role in 'building global community'. This is a populist, not a democratic, formulation. Facebook lacks a normative view of democracy, is prepared to make political accommodations in the interest of its business and offers a platform for those opposed to the kind of liberal democracy which brought Facebook into being.[4]

Democracy demands more than efforts to safeguard the security of elections: it demands support for democratic institutions. Facebook stands implicated as a platform for state-sponsored cyber-warfare, terrorism, hate speech, child abuse, human rights abuses and even genocide.

Facebook, elections and referendums

Ian Lucas MP, a critical voice on the House of Commons DCMS Select Committee, has said, 'Facebook is the most important platform in election campaigns in the UK.' Facebook facilitates data-driven electioneering: building the audience, segmenting it, message creation and testing, message targeting and delivery and fundraising. The Trump campaign spent an estimated \$70–90 million on Facebook advertising and raised \$250–280 million.[5] Facebook staff were embedded in the Trump and Clinton campaigns to assist campaign operatives in their targeting.[6]

The importance of Facebook advertising for the Trump campaign has been emphasised by Campaign Director Steve Bannon and others. Sophisticated advertising techniques were utilised to test and market different variations of advertisements to different demographic groups and in different geographic areas. Data analytics teams, including staff from Cambridge Analytica, used 5,000 data points on 200 million Americans, to target advertising, raise funds and schedule events and determine in which states to focus campaign efforts, including a specific focus on Michigan, Wisconsin and Pennsylvania in the last few days of the campaign. The data of 30 million US citizens obtained by Cambridge Analytica was used in the US election. The chair of the DCMS Select Committee, Damian Collins, MP, has said that the UK Information Commissioner had found evidence that data had been accessed from Russia. The political communications specialist Kathleen Hall Jamieson has demonstrated how the Trump and Russian campaigns reinforced one another's targeting.[7]

The most important tools used by the Trump campaign were Facebook's standard advertising offerings – Custom Audiences, loading in all known Trump supporters and segmenting them by race, gender, location and other attributes; then the Lookalike Audiences tool to find people with similar interests and qualities; and testing advertising using other Facebook marketing tools. Negative advertising was developed to suppress voting turnout by demographic groups or areas likely to be sympathetic to Hillary Clinton. These were often personally targeted and invisible to other users ('dark posts' and 'dark ads'). The provocative Trump ads may have drawn more engagement, pushing down their cost. In its answer to the Senate on these issues, Facebook merely says that it offered 'identical support' to both campaigns.[8]

The UK's referendum on Brexit was a test-bed. Roger McNamee has said, 'it seemed likely that Facebook might have had a big impact on the vote because one side's message was perfect for the algorithms and the other's wasn't'. The *Observer*'s award-winning journalist Carole Cadwalladr was the first to point to the role of an obscure Canadian digital advertising and software company AggregateIQ and its links with the Leave campaign. The UK Information Commissioner (ICO) subsequently found that Aggregate IQ had significant links to Cambridge Analytica.[9]

AggregateIQ placed significant numbers of advertisements on Facebook for Leave: about 1 billion targeted advertisements were served, mainly on

Facebook. Different versions were tested. For some time, AggregateIQ carried a testimonial on its website from the campaign director of the official Vote Leave campaign, Dominic Cummings:

> Without doubt, the Vote Leave campaign owes a great deal of its success to AggregateIQ. We couldn't have done it without them.[10]

Cummings himself has said that UK electoral laws are not fit for the digital age. The various Leave campaigns, official and unofficial, have been fined for election law and data law breaches, and there is a National Crime Agency investigation into the sources of funding of one of the campaigns. One prominent British academic has testified that overspending by the various Leave campaigns could have swayed the Brexit vote in the UK. All of these issues have been the subject of legislative inquiries in the US, the UK, Canada and the European Parliament.[11]

There is nothing wrong with political parties using Facebook advertising. Earlier campaigns, such as Obama's 2012 presidential campaign, had developed sophisticated data targeting operations, which were closely integrated with Facebook's systems, though there is no suggestion that they contracted with any parties who illicitly had access to Facebook data.[12]

The issue of micro-targeting, of dark advertising and dark posts paid for by dark money, where adverts are seen by limited groups of people and the source and its funding are not declared, has become a significant focus of concern. Traditionally, there has been relative transparency in political advertising, and it has been regulated. Key to this has been identifying the source of the advertising on print, on posters and in other media. Facebook, under pressure, has begun to make changes, compelling political advertisers to have their advertisements pre-authorised, so that identity and location can be confirmed, making advertising more transparent by publishing who has paid for it and ensuring that ads being run from Facebook pages are visible to all through an archive. Legislation on this has happened in Canada and Australia and is planned in the UK.[13]

Added to this is the sheer scale and sophistication afforded by big data analytics to test messages in volume and target precisely. Facebook has run its own campaigns to encourage voter turnout: research suggests that its 'nudges' can be very effective. There is no transparency about how it chooses where to mount these turnout campaigns. Given the concerns that exist around Facebook's attempts to manipulate user emotions, it is no wonder that Facebook's potential power as a political actor should prompt demands for tighter regulation.[14]

Facebook and national security

In January 2017, the three US intelligence agencies concluded that Russian President Vladimir Putin ordered a campaign in 2016 to undermine public faith in the US democratic process, denigrate Secretary of State Hillary Clinton and harm her electability. They added 'we further assess Putin and the Russian Government developed a clear preference for President-elect Trump'. In April, Facebook published a security report on interference in the elections. Facebook later admitted cutting out references to Russia, because of concerns from its legal and policy teams. In the autumn of 2018, Facebook came under further pressure about the internal discussions which had taken place over what to publish, when the *New York Times* suggested that these had led to serious divisions at the top of the company.[15]

Facebook conceded in September 2017 that Russian sources had spent about $100,000 on Facebook advertising in the run up to the 2016 election. They handed over 3,000 election advertisements paid for by Kremlin-linked actors, including by the Russian 'troll factory', the Internet Research Agency. Facebook estimated that 10 million people might have seen the advertisements. Research by Dr Jonathan Albright subsequently showed that these advertisements, which included classic voter suppression and racially divisive advertising, might have been shared hundreds of millions of times, although before he could complete his research, Facebook removed access to the data sets on which he had been working. Instagram is not excluded from this. Dr Albright identified 170 Instagram accounts spreading Russian propaganda compared to 120 Facebook pages. Facebook owned up that Russian 'memes' might have reached 126 million people, some spread by trolls and 'sock-puppets'.[16]

In February 2018, Special Counsel Robert Mueller handed down indictments to several Russian operatives in a case against the Internet Research Agency amongst others which stated, 'the defendants and their co-conspirators also created thematic group pages on social media sites, particularly on the social media platforms Facebook and Instagram'. These weren't just advertisements: some stimulated people into action, such as marches and rallies.[17]

In July 2018, Mark Zuckerberg confirmed that Facebook had known since 2015 about Russian attempts by the group Advanced Persistent Threat (APT) 28 to abuse the platform.[18] As far as Russian interference in Brexit is concerned, there has been no Mueller equivalent. A Minority Staff report for the US Senate Committee on Foreign Relations found that

> the picture of potential Russian meddling in the June referendum vote
> has only begun to come into sharper focus as subsequent elections

around the world revealed common elements – false or inflammatory stories circulated by bots and trolls.

Facebook has confirmed to the UK House of Commons that there were Russia-linked ads during the Brexit referendum campaign.[19]

Terrorism

Facebook has spoken relatively openly of its work to stop the spread of Islamist terrorism on its network, explaining how it uses machine learning to detect the bulk of ISIS- or al-Qaeda-related material. Facebook says that it has reduced the amount of time reported material stays online significantly, though it regards amount of exposure as more important than duration. Facebook works with law enforcement agencies across the world and through the Global Internet Forum to Combat Terrorism, which includes Microsoft, Twitter and YouTube. Digital 'fingerprints' or 'hashes' (image, video, audio and text) of identified terrorist material are shared with these other providers to permit earlier detection and removal. Millions of pieces of terrorist material were taken down in 2018 alone.

The disinformation researcher Renee DiResta says that social networks 'facilitated' ISIS's online activities, 'simultaneously providing a captive user base, a virality engine infrastructure, no editorial oversight, and fairly limited rules'.

What ISIS pioneered, she says, Russia learned: essentially, how to exploit 'a relatively lawless federated system for reaching mass audiences'. While others were focused on Facebook's 'fake news problem', DiResta was already warning about the radicalisation effects of Facebook Groups:

> If you join a Facebook Group for a particular topic, it will naturally serve you other Groups, Pages, and news content related to that topic. Join a couple more, and it'll look at the people who are common to the groups, decide that you are probably something like them, and then suggest other Groups based on groups that *they* are in.[20]

Interrogating Facebook data is difficult, and data on private groups is not available, Professor Pete Burnap of Cardiff University's Hatelab explained to me, so it is not possible to track with confidence the interactions within them. The Counter-Extremism Project has documented in detail how Facebook's algorithms have connected ISIS terrorists and potential recruits together, making recommendations of people to friend and groups to join. In other words, this is a systemic problem, directly linked to Facebook's business model.[21]

Far-right movements and white nationalist terrorism

Facebook has aided the growth of far-right white nationalist and neo-Nazi movements across the world. Donna Zuckerberg says, 'the election of Donald Trump in 2016 empowered these online communities to be even more outspoken about their ideology'. Breitbart, says Martin Moore, acts as a bridge between the alt-right and neo-Nazi sites in the US. Daniel Kreiss calls it 'the supporting media for a contemporary white nationalist cultural commune that falls under the label of the alt-right'. Facebook was critical to Breitbart's success, Steve Bannon has said. Behavioural scientists working for the UK security service MI5 have warned 'social media provides a forum in which people can explore their dark thoughts in the company of like-minded people'. Extreme and polarising views have been amplified into the mainstream, with Facebook central to this.[22]

Facebook has been the central communication platform for extreme right organisations like the English Defence League (EDL), Britain First and the extremist leader Stephen Yaxley-Lennon, also known as Tommy Robinson, as well as extreme right movements in mainland Europe. When he was banned from Facebook and Instagram in 2019, Yaxley-Lennon had a following of one million people. Britain First and the EDL gained additional social media support after the terrorist murder of British soldier Lee Rigby on the streets of London in May 2013. Cardiff University research has shown that multiple social media platforms, including Facebook, were used to spread disinformation following the 2017 UK terrorist attacks.

The EDL and Britain First both used emotional videos and tabloid-style clickbait posts about immigration and Islam mixed with stories supportive of Britain's troops and remembrance activities to draw in unsuspecting innocent supporters as part of their strategy of building support. Pai notes how Britain First managed to lead many people to become engaged without realising what sort of organisation it was. This approach, as Donna Zuckerberg explains, is

> a conversion process . . . often called 'swallowing the red pill' – a reference to the famous scene in the film The Matrix (1999) in which Morpheus (Laurence Fishburne) offers Neo (Keanu Reeves) a choice to return to blissful ignorance or learn the truth about their reality.

Disinformation may be inculcated on sites like 4chan or Reddit and move to Twitter; then, if it is starting to get media traction, it moves to the mass market, which is Facebook, where it is placed in Facebook groups to ensure widespread sharing and acceptance. Rebecca Lewis and Alice Marwick describe red-pilling thus:

> In far-right circles, one is redpilled when they begin believing a truth that is counterfactual to a mainstream belief, which may include white supremacy, Holocaust denial, the danger that immigration posits for white Americans, the oppression of men by feminists, and so forth.

The Pizzagate conspiracy theory, which was based on the idea that a supposed Democratic Party paedophile ring operated out of pizza restaurants in Washington, DC, and resulted in one individual firing shots into a specific pizza restaurant in December 2016, developed in this way. The right-wing terrorist who killed a man and injured others in Finsbury Park in 2017 was also radicalised by social media.[23]

A Channel Four documentary on Facebook moderation procedures in 2018 showed a manager in the moderation team saying that the page of the far-right UK leader Tommy Robinson, which had been found to have violated Facebook's community guidelines, would have to be referred up because of the number of followers he had. This suggested that Facebook's concern was actually to maintain sites that had large numbers of followers in order to keep monetising them in the US; it was only in the summer of 2018 that the far-right conspiracy theorist behind Infowars found his Facebook page taken down.[24]

In March 2019, Facebook finally banned white nationalist groups and propaganda from its site, and specific named groups and individuals were subsequently banned. The decision came two weeks after a white nationalist terrorist attacked two mosques in Christchurch, New Zealand, killing 50 worshippers. He had announced the attack on the 8chan message-board and live-streamed it on Facebook. Facebook tried to stop viewing of the video, stating it was viewed live fewer than 200 times and about 4,000 times in total before being removed. In the first 24 hours, Facebook removed about 1.5 million videos of the attack globally, with 1.2 million blocked at upload. Alex Stamos, former chief security officer of Facebook, says combatting white nationalist terrorism is different from combatting ISIS, as there is a network of smaller platforms such as 8chan, which allow white supremacist content to proliferate, and the penalties imposed by governments on groups hosting ISIS content do not exist for these.[25]

Days after the attack, UK Digital Minister Margot James said that it called into question the role of live-streaming services. In April, Facebook banned the British extreme-right groups the BNP, EDL and Britain First. Later that month, a Facebook executive confessed to the UK Parliament that Facebook's systems had failed to identify the video for blocking immediately because in events before this 'we had not seen content from the actual angle of the shooter or the attacker'. Inconsistencies in Facebook's policies are still being found.[26]

Facebook and international human rights

In 2013, Mark Zuckerberg asked, 'Is connectivity a human right?' In his own mind, it was. He announced a plan 'to sustainably provide free access to basic internet services'. What sprang from that were internet.org and the Free Basics platform on which the services sat. It has had some success – 100 million people connected in 70 countries. In many countries, Facebook is the Internet: surveys have shown that people don't even know that using Facebook means they are technically on the Internet.[27] In rolling out its service, Facebook has run into resistance from net neutrality and anti-colonial activists and from regulators like the Telecommunications Regulatory Authority of India.[28]

Little thought seems to have been given to the negative externalities, or to the systems and processes of management, policy and governance that Facebook would need to have in place. 'Facebook is an idealistic and optimistic company', Mark Zuckerberg told Congress in 2018, but it is the morality of a 2016 memo written by Facebook senior executive Andrew 'Boz' Bosworth – 'The Ugly' – that comes to mind here:

> Maybe someone dies in a terrorist attack coordinated on our tools. . . .
> We connect people. Period. That's why all the work we do in growth
> is justified.

The human right of connectivity has caused the breaching of other human rights.

In August 2018, the United Nations Independent International Fact-Finding Mission on Myanmar reported on a range of human rights atrocities, including crimes against humanity bordering on genocide of the Rohingya people:

> Facebook has been a useful instrument for those seeking to spread hate,
> in a context where for most users Facebook *is* the Internet. Although
> improved in recent months, Facebook's response has been slow and
> ineffective. The extent to which Facebook posts and messages have led
> to real-world discrimination and violence must be independently and
> thoroughly examined.[29]

Facebook had not employed a single Burmese-speaker until 2015, had no staff in Myanmar and monitored hate speech online from an outsourced monitoring operation in Kuala Lumpur. Initially, it only had one Burmese-speaker in its moderation team, based in Dublin. This grew to four people, based in Dublin and Manila, at a time when there were 7.3 million active Facebook users in Myanmar.

On the day the UN published the report from its mission, Facebook banned 20 organisations and individuals in Myanmar, including a military leader.[30]

Facebook commissioned the corporate social responsibility consultancy BSR to carry out an independent assessment of its activity in Myanmar. The report confirmed the findings of the UN mission that Facebook had allowed hate speech to flourish and had become a platform through which violence was incited. There were significant implications for Facebook's governance and accountability, including human rights policies, formalised governance structures and public communications and, tellingly, community standards *enforcement* by Facebook. Facebook's investment in local country staff was unlikely to be unique to Myanmar. There was cynicism about Facebook's motivation in taking action, with the view being expressed that Facebook was more concerned about its reputation on Capitol Hill.[31]

Facebook's 'privacy pivot' and the coming encryption wars

The BSR report looked ahead to future challenges that Facebook might face, particularly if WhatsApp, which is an encrypted messaging service, became widely available in Myanmar. Fake news issues are prevalent on Facebook services, including WhatsApp, in other countries, including Kenya and Nigeria. Neo-Nazi propaganda has been spread on WhatsApp in Germany. In India, Facebook has been challenged over the role of What-sApp in a series of lynchings across the country, based on misinformation spread across the platform. Facebook has taken steps to limit certain kinds of WhatsApp features. Stories that are forwarded are now labelled as such; limits were put on the number of stories which can be forwarded and suspicious stories are flagged. WhatsApp's role in elections in Brazil has also come under scrutiny, where the app has 120 million users, with Facebook taking down 100,000 fake accounts.[32]

Mark Zuckerberg's announcement in early 2019 that Facebook would in future focus more on private communications via encrypted apps and participation in groups poses further worrying challenges for the rule of law, democracy, human rights and counter-terrorism. But many people suggest this is a way of Facebook evading the long-term costs of content moderation. If the content is encrypted and can't be read, then it will be harder to hold Facebook accountable for it.[33]

Governments will always want easier access to encrypted terrorist messages, but as a number of authors have pointed out, weakening end-to-end encryption through the use of electronic backdoors means weakening encryption for everyone. Government agencies through court orders have anyway found ways through this. Some point out in any case that if there were weaker encryption, then users would move to other alternatives. Former FBI Director James Comey reports discussing encryption with President Obama. The president told him, 'You know, this is really hard. . . . Normally I can figure these things out, but this one is really hard.'[34]

What isn't hard to understand is that Facebook profits from dark advertising, disinformation campaigns, terrorism, crime and hate speech, and authoritarianism.

Notes

1 Quoted in Facebook's 2012 IPO Filing, www.sec.gov/Archives/edgar/data/1326801/000119312512034517/d287954ds1.htm#toc287954_10.
2 Lev Grossman, *Time*, 15 December 2010, http://content.time.com/time/specials/packages/article/0,28804,2036683_2037183_2037185,00.html.
3 Mark Zuckerberg, *Building Global Community*, 12 February 2017, www.facebook.com/notes/mark-zuckerberg/building-global-community/10154544292806634; Olivia Solon, Facebook's Fake News: Mark Zuckerberg Rejects 'Crazy Idea' That It Swayed Voters, *Guardian*, 11 November 2016, www.theguardian.com/technology/2016/nov/10/facebook-fake-news-us-election-mark-zuckerberg-donald-trump.
4 Fattal, 2012: 945, 951; Jørgensen, 2018: 344; Kreiss and McGregor, 2018: 20.
5 Ian Lucas MP's comment from author's personal note, 18 March 2019; Baldwin-Philippi, 2017; Karpf, 2017; Tambini, 2018: 274; Kreiss and McGregor, 2017; Moore, 2019. I have seen estimates of $70 or $90 million: Sue Halpern, How He Used Facebook to Win, *New York Review of Books*, 8 June 2017, www.nybooks.com/articles/2017/06/08/how-trump-used-facebook-to-win/; Issie Lapowsky, Here's How Facebook Actually Won Trump the Presidency, *Wired*, 15 November 2016, www.wired.com/2016/11/facebook-won-trump-election-not-just-fake-news/.
6 Facebook announced in September 2018 that it was scrapping this practice, which has of course made money for the company: see Facebook Stops Sending Staff to Help Political Campaigns, *BBC News*, 21 September 2018, www.bbc.co.uk/news/technology-45599962; on Facebook's financial benefit from 'embedding', see Campaign for Accountability, *Partisan Programming: How Facebook and Google's Campaign Embeds Benefit Their Bottom Lines*, August 2018, https://campaignforaccountability.org/work/partisan-programming-how-facebook-and-googles-campaign-embeds-benefit-their-bottom-lines/.
7 The effectiveness of 'psychographics' or psychological profiling is disputed, and Cambridge Analytica said that it had not used psychographics in the Trump campaign: see Nicholas Confessore and Danny Hakim, Data Firm Says 'Secret Sauce' Aided Trump; Many Scoff, *New York Times*, 6 May 2017, www.nytimes.com/2017/03/06/us/politics/cambridge-analytica.html, and Bartlett, 2018: 88;

Vaidhyanathan, 2018, 150–158, 169–172; Trump's campaign director, Steve Bannon, has acknowledged the power of Facebook: 'I wouldn't have come aboard, even for Trump, if I hadn't known they were building this massive Facebook and data engine. Facebook is what propelled Breitbart to a massive audience. We knew its power,' in Alexis C. Madrigal, What Facebook Did to American Democracy, *The Atlantic*, 12 October 2017, www.theatlantic.com/technology/archive/2017/10/what-facebook-did/542502/; one Trump campaign operative, working alongside Cambridge Analytica, said 'without Facebook we wouldn't have won', Jamie Bartlett, Big Data Is Watching You, *Spectator*, 24 March 2018, 14–15; BBC, 2017, The Secrets of Silicon Valley (presented by Bartlett) available at www.bbc.co.uk/programmes/b0916ghq; on the accessing of the data from Russia, see Press Association, Facebook data gathered by Cambridge Analytica accessed from Russia, says MP, *Guardian*, 18 July, www.theguardian.com/technology/2018/jul/18/facebook-data-gathered-by-cambridge-analytica-accessed-from-russia-says-mp-damian-collins; Hall Jamieson, 2018.

8 Tambini, 2018; on dark advertising in British campaigns, see Carole Cadwalladr, Revealed: How Tory Attack Ads Targeted Voters' Facebook Feeds in a Marginal Seat, *Observer*, 29 May 2017, 5; Mark Ritson, How to Win an Election in Seven Complex Steps, *Marketing Week*, 5 June 2017, www.marketingweek.com/2017/06/05/mark-ritson-how-win-election/; Casey Newton, How Facebook Rewards Polarizing Political Ads, *The Verge*, 11 October 2017, www.theverge.com/2017/10/11/16449976/facebook-political-ads-trump-russia-election-news-feed; A.G. Martinez, How Trump Conquered Facebook Without Russian Ads, *Wired*, 23 February 2018, www.wired.com/story/how-trump-conquered-facebookwithout-russian-ads/; Brian Feldman, Did Facebook Really Charge Trump Less for Advertising? *New York Magazine*, 28 February 2018, http://nymag.com/selectall/2018/02/the-truth-about-facebook-cpms-donald-trump-and-digital-ads.html. For Facebook's replies to Senate follow-up questions, 11 June 2018, www.commerce.senate.gov/public/_cache/files/9d8e069d-2670-4530-bcdc-d3a63a8831c4/7C8DE61421D13E86FC6855CC2EA7AEA7.senate-commerce-committee-combined-qfrs-06.11.2018.pdf.

9 Roger McNamee, How to Fix Facebook – Before It Fixes Us, *Washington Monthly*, January–March 2018, https://washingtonmonthly.com/magazine/january-february-march-2018/how-to-fix-facebook-before-it-fixes-us/; see Carole Cadwalladr, Cambridge Analytica Has Gone: But What Is Left in Its Wake? *Observer*, 6 May 2018, for a summary, www.theguardian.com/uk-news/2018/may/06/cambridge-analytica-gone-what-has-it-left-in-its-wake; also see Carole Cadwalladr, Exposing Cambridge Analytica: It's Been Exhausting, Exhilarating, and Slightly Terrifying, 29 September 2018, www.theguardian.com/membership/2018/sep/29/cambridge-analytica-cadwalladr-observer-facebook-zuckerberg-wylie; ICO, 2018c; Issie Lapowsky, Shadow Politics: Meet the Digital Sleuth Exposing Fake News, *Wired*, 18 July 2018, www.wired.com/story/shadow-politics-meet-the-digital-sleuth-exposing-fake-news/.

10 On Aggregate IQ and the Brexit campaign, see Carole Cadwalladr, Cambridge Analytica Affairs Raises Questions Vital to Our Democracy, 4 March 2017, www.theguardian.com/politics/2017/mar/04/cambridge-analytica-democracy-digital-age; The Great British Brexit Robbery: How a Secret Network of Computer Scientists Hijacked Our Democracy, *Observer*, The New Review, 7 May 2017, 12–15, 'Follow the Data: Is This the Document That Connects

the Brexit Campaigns to a US Billionaire – and Blows a Hole in Our Democracy? *Observer*, 14 May 2017, 14–15 and Brexit Insider Claims Vote Leave Team 'May Have Broken Law', *Observer*, 25 March 2018, 1, 5, and 'In a Country Where My Decision as a Voter Matters, This Is a Huge Deal' Leave Campaigner Turned Whistle-Blower, Shahmir Sanni, *Observer*, The New Review, 25 March 2018, 8–13; For Vote Leave's endorsement, see https://aggregateiq. com/2017, last accessed 30 March 2018; see also Patrick Foster and Martin Evans, Tiny Canadian Firm That Swung Result for the Brexit Camp, *Daily Telegraph*, 25 February 2017, 6–7.

11 The UK's Electoral Commission fined Leave campaign organisations, including Vote Leave, and passed further evidence to the police: Electoral Commission, 2018; Information Commissioner's Office, 2018a, 2018b and 2018c and 2019; See Toby Helm, Was the Brexit Poll Compromised? We May Need a Public Debate About That, *Observer*, 15 April, 2018, 12–13; How the World Was Trolled, *Economist*, 4 November 2017, 21–25; Dominic Cummings, On the Referendum #22: Some Basic Numbers for the Vote Leave Campaign, 2018, https:// dominiccummings.com/on-the-eu-referendum/, last accessed 1 October 2018; see also Paul Hilder, The Revolution Will Be Digitised, *Prospect*, May 2017, 32–38; Carole Cadwalladr, The Great British Brexit Robbery: How a Secret Network of Computer Scientists Hijacked Our Democracy, *Observer*, The New Review, 7 May 2017, 12–15; on the impact of the overspend, see Howard, 2018. One of the other Leave campaigns, Leave.EU, and its chief funder Arron Banks's company Eldon Insurance, has subsequently been fined by the Information Commissioner's Office for illegal data-sharing. The ICO has now concluded that Leave.EU's relationship with Cambridge Analytica, on whose board sat Trump adviser Steve Bannon, and which was funded by right-wing billionaire Robert Mercer, who also funded Breitbart News which Bannon ran, ended at an early stage; see Carole Cadwalladr, Arron Banks, the insurers, and my strange data trail, *Observer*, 22 April 2018, 34–36; see Paul Lewis and Paul Hilder, Data Firm 'Misled MPs' Over Work for Brexit Campaign, *Guardian*, 24 March 2018, 1;Carole Cadwalladr, Arron Banks, Leave EU and Fresh Questions Over Funding of Referendum Campaign, *Observer*, 15 April 2018, 13; Tom Metcalf and Stephanie Baker, The Mysterious Finances of Brexit Campaign's Biggest Backer, *Bloomberg*, 24 February 2019, www.bloomberg.com/news/ features/2019-02-24/brexit-backer-aaron-banks-how-much-is-he-worth. The Cambridge Analytica denial that it used Facebook data in the Trump campaign can be found at the end of this article: Hannes Grassegger and Mikael Krogerus, The Data That Turned the World Upside Down, 28 January 2017, https:// motherboard.vice.com/en_us/article/mg9vvn/how-our-likes-helped-trump-win: on the alt-right political networks, see Jonathan Albright, The #Election2016 Micro-Propaganda Machine, *Medium*, 18 November 2016, https://medium. com/@d1gi/the-election2016-micro-propaganda-machine-383449cc1fba and Carole Cadwalladr, The Great British Brexit Robbery: How a Secret Network of Computer Scientists Hijacked Our Democracy, *Observer*, The New Review, 7 May 2017, 12–15; on SCL, Cambridge Analytica and Leave.EU, see the evidence from Dr Emma L. Briant to the House of Commons DCMS Select Committee, 16 April 2018, www.parliament.uk/business/committees/committees-a-z/commons-select/digital-culture-media-and-sport-committee/news/ fake-news-briant-evidence-17-19/; Brexit-related dark advertising continues: Jim Waterson, Facebook Brexit Ads Secretly Run by Staff of Lynton Crosby

Firm, *Guardian*, 3 April 2019, www.theguardian.com/politics/2019/apr/03/grassroots-facebook-brexit-ads-secretly-run-by-staff-of-lynton-crosby-firm.

12 Tufekci, 2014; Kreiss, 2017; see also Dave Denison interview with Siva Vaidhyanathan, The Zuckerberg Follies, *The Baffler*, 4 June 2018, https://thebaffler.com/latest/the-zuckerberg-follies-denison ; Ben Thompson, The Facebook Brand, *Stratechery*, 19 March 2018, https://stratechery.com/2018/the-facebook-brand/.

13 For 'stealth media', see Kim et al. (2018); Josh Constine, Facebook and Instagram Launch US Political Ad Labelling and Archive, *Techcrunch*, 24 May 2018, https://techcrunch.com/2018/05/24/facebook-political-ad-archive/; David Ingram, Facebook, in Reversal, to Publish Cache of Political Ads, *Reuters*, 27 October 2017, www.reuters.com/article/us-facebook-advertising/facebook-in-reversal-to-publish-cache-of-political-ads-idUSKBN1CW2LG; on Obama's campaign engagement with Facebook, see Dan Balz, How the Obama Campaign Won the Race for Data, *Washington Post*, 28 July 2013, www.washingtonpost.com/politics/how-the-obama-campaign-won-the-race-for-voter-data/2013/07/28/ad32c7b4-ee4e-11e2-a1f9-ea873b7e0424_story.html?utm_term=.5e14745a7a75.

14 Kreiss, 2017; ICO, 2018b. Researchers have demonstrated that Facebook targeting lifted turnout by a margin that was significant (Bond et al., 2012; Jones et al., 2017). Facebook has subsequently used voter turnout encouragement in elections and referendums in a variety of other countries, including the Scottish referendum in 2014, the Irish referendum of 2015, the UK 2015 General Election, the 2016 EU referendum in the UK and the US presidential election in 2016. See also Jonathan Zittrain, Facebook Could Decide an Election Without Anyone Ever Finding Out, *The New Republic*, 2 June 2014, https://newrepublic.com/article/117878/information-fiduciary-solution-facebook-digital-gerrymandering; Hannes Graggerus, Facebook Says Its 'Voter Button' Is Good for Turnout: But Should the Tech Giant Be Nudging Us at All? *Observer*, The New Review, 15 April 2018, 20–23; Sam Biddle, Facebook Quietly Hid Pages Bragging of Ability to Influence Elections, *The Intercept*, 14 March 2018, https://theintercept.com/2018/03/14/facebook-election-meddling/; Facebook conducted an 'emotional contagion' experiment on 689,003 users along with researchers at Cornell University, in which positive posts from friends were partially withheld from one group and negative posts from another. Cardiff University psychology professor Chris Chambers challenged the ethical conduct of a study which had been carried out without informed consent, saying that the case pointed out how 'unregulated' consumer marketing research was: Chris Chambers, Facebook Fiasco: Was Cornell's 'Emotional Contagion Study' an Ethics Breach?' *Guardian*, 1 July 2014, www.theguardian.com/science/head-quarters/2014/jul/01/facebook-cornell-study-emotional-contagion-ethics-breach. Facebook itself has announced a major project to look at the impact of social media on elections, in partnership with academics and a number of foundations – Elliott Schrage and David Ginsberg, Facebook Launches New Initiative to Help Scholars Assess Social Media's Impact on Elections, 9 April 2018, https://newsroom.fb.com/news/2018/04/new-elections-initiative/.

15 Office of the Director of National Intelligence, 2017. Background to 'Assessing Russian Activities and Intentions in Recent US Elections': The Analytic Process and Cyber Incident Attribution, www.intelligence.senate.gov/sites/default/files/documents/ICA_2017_01.pdf; Jen Weedon, William Nuland and Alex Stamos,

Information Operations and Facebook, *Facebook Newsroom*, 27 April 2017, https://fbnewsroomus.files.wordpress.com/2017/04/facebook-and-informa tion-operations-v1.pdf; Alex Stamos, An Update on Security Operations on Facebook, https://newsroom.fb.com/news/2017/09/information-operations-update/; *Facebook Newsroom*, 6 September 2017, https://newsroom.fb.com/news/2017/09/information-operations-update/; Sheera Frenkel, Nicholas Confessore, Cecilia Kang, Matthew Rosenberg and Jack Nicas, Delay, Deny and Deflect: How Facebook's Leaders Fought Through Crisis, *New York Times*, 14 November 2018, www.nytimes.com/2018/11/14/technology/facebook-data-russia-election-racism.html; Facebook's Sheryl Sandberg to CBS: We Absolutely Did Not Pay Anyone to Create Fake News, *CBS News*, 16 November 2018, www.cbsnews.com/news/sheryl-sandberg-facebook-coo-we-absolutely-did-not-pay-anyone-to-create-fake-news/. Facebook's head of security, Alex Stamos, subsequently announced that he was to leave the company. Press reports said that he had sought greater disclosure over the impact of Russian interference in the Facebook platform.

16 Craig Timberg, Russian Propaganda May Have Been Shared Hundreds of Millions of Times, *Washington Post*, 5 October 2017, www.washingtonpost.com/news/the-switch/wp/2017/10/05/russian-propaganda-may-have-been-shared-hundreds-of-millions-of-times-new-research-says/; Craig Timberg and Elizabeth Dwoskin, Facebook Takes Down Data and Thousands of Posts Obscuring Reach of Russian Disinformation, *Washington Post*, 12 October 2017, www.washingtonpost.com/news/the-switch/wp/2017/10/12/facebook-takes-down-data-and-thousands-of-posts-obscuring-reach-of-russian-disinformation/?utm_term=.4df601a86140; George Washington University professor Dave Karpf warned that some of these shares and views might themselves have been by bots, so it was difficult to be accurate about how many humans had seen the advertising: People are hyperventilating over a study of Russian propaganda on Facebook. Just breathe deeply, *Washington Post*, 12 October 2018, www.washingtonpost.com/news/monkey-cage/wp/2017/10/12/people-are-hyperventilating-over-a-new-study-of-russian-propaganda-on-facebook-just-breathe-deeply/?utm_term=.2cf3739b2ec7; Robert McMillan and Shane Harris, Facebook Cut Russia Out of April Report on Election Influence, *Wall Street Journal*, 5 October 2017, www.wsj.com/articles/facebook-cut-russia-out-of-april-report-on-election-influence-1507253503.

17 The full indictment issued by the District Court for the District of Columbia on behalf of Special Counsel Robert Mueller can be read here: www.nytimes.com/interactive/2018/02/16/us/politics/document-The-Special-Counsel-s-Indict ment-of-the-Internet.html: see also David Smith, Putin's Chief, the Troll Farm in St Petersburg, and the Plot to Hijack US Democracy, *Observer*, 18 February 2018, 8; Hannah Kuchler, America Versus the Hackers, *FTCOM/Magazine*, 28–29 April 2018, 22–25.

18 Kara Swisher, Full Transcript: Facebook CEO Mark Zuckerberg on Recode Decode, 18 July 2018, www.recode.net/2018/7/18/17575158/mark-zuckerberg-facebook-interview-full-transcript-kara-swisher.

19 Russian objectives are to split EU and NATO and destabilise western democracies, stirring up division, building on the so-called 2013 'Gerasimov doctrine' of total warfare, named after the chief of the Russian general staff. For a good summary of Russian cyberwarfare activity, including the Gerasimov doctrine, see Hannes Grassegger and Mikael Krogerus, Fake News and Botnets: How

Russia Weaponised the Web, *Observer*, New Review, 3 December 2017, 17–19 and Andrew Kramer, Russian General Pitches 'Information' Operations as a Form of War, *New York Times*, 2 March 2019, www.nytimes.com/2019/03/02/world/europe/russia-hybrid-war-gerasimov.html; Mathew Ingram, Fake News Is Part of a Bigger Problem: Automated Propaganda, *Columbia Journalism Review*, 22 February 2018, www.cjr.org/analysis/algorithm-russia-facebook.php; Patrick, 2017, especially 28–32, 139–161, 261; Vaidhyanathan, 180, 186–8; Carole Cadwalladr, Trump, Assange, Bannon, Farage . . . Bound Together in an Unholy Alliance, *Observer*, 29 October 2017, 33; Carole Cadwalladr, Top Brexit Funder Had Multiple Meetings with Russian Officials, *Observer*, 10 June 2018, 1, 7 and Aaron Banks, Brexit and the Kremlin Connection, *Observer*, 17 June 2018, 35–37; Richard Kerbaj, Caroline Wheeler, Tim Shipman and Tom Harper, Revealed: Brexit Backer's Golden Kremlin Connection, *Sunday Times*, 10 June, 2018, 1–3; Nick Cohen, Why Isn't There Greater Outrage About Russia's Involvement in Brexit? *Observer*, 17 June 2018, 52. For wider contextualisation, see Tamsin Shaw, The New Military-Industrial Complex of Big Data Psy-Ops, *New York Review of Books*, 21 March 2018, www.nybooks.com/daily/2018/03/21/the-digital-military-industrial-complex/; Michael Schwirtz and Sheera Frenkel, In Ukraine, Russia Tests a New Facebook Tactic in Election Tampering, *New York Times*, 29 March 2019, www.nytimes.com/2019/03/29/world/europe/ukraine-russia-election-tampering-propaganda.html; House of Commons, 2018a; US Senate, 2018.

20 Sunstein, 2017: 238; Tweet by Zeynep Tufekci, 10 March 2018, https://twitter.com/zeynep/status/972591994659745792?lang=en; Renee diResta, How ISIS and Russia Won Friends and Manufactured Crowds, *Wired*, 8 March 2018, www.wired.com/story/isis-russia-manufacture-crowds/, and Up Next: A Better Recommendation Engine, *Wired*, 11 April 2018, www.wired.com/story/creating-ethical-recommendation-engines/ and Fake News and Rabbit-Holes: Radicalization via the Recommendation Engine, *Medium*, 13 November 2016, https://medium.com/the-graph/fake-news-and-rabbit-holes-radicalization-via-the-recommendation-engine-544f99337c55.

21 Counter-Extremism Project, 2018; Author's notes of conversation with Professor Pete Burnap, 4 March 2019.

22 Jessica Elgot, Boris Johnson Accused of 'Dog-Whistle' Islamophobia Over Burqa Comments, *Guardian*, 6 August 2018, www.theguardian.com/politics/2018/aug/06/boris-johnsons-burqa-remarks-fan-flames-of-islamophobia-says-mp; Stephen Bush, Boris Johnson's Meeting with Steve Bannon Is a Sign of His Real Character, *New Statesman*, 26 July 2018, www.newstatesman.com/politics/elections/2018/07/boris-johnson-s-meeting-steve-bannon-sign-his-true-character; Caroline Wheeler, Tommy Walters and Felix Forbes, Racists Flock to Boris on Facebook, *Sunday Times*, 19 August 2018, 1; Richard Kerbaj, Social Media Are Like a School for Terrorists, Say MI5 Experts, *Daily Telegraph*, 24 February 2019, 20.

23 CREST, 2017; Zuckerberg, D, 2018; Kreiss, 2018: 14; see Stocker, 2017; danah boyd, 2018; Bartlett and Littler, 2011; Bartlett et al., 2011; Bartlett and Krasodomski-Jones, 2015, 2016; Kassimeris and Jackson, 2015; Alessio and Meredith, 2013; Allen, 2011; Howard, 2015: 216, 219; Ernst et al., 2017; Lewis and Marwick, 2017; Marwick does however warn (2018) that red-pilling can be viewed in a similar way to the hypodermic needle model of ideas transmission. The work of organisations like Hope not Hate and the Institute for

Strategic Dialogue is essential on 4chan and its mutually reinforcing relationship with Fox News, see Phillips, 2013. For Pizzagate- see McNamee, 2019: 124–125; Tristan Kirk, Anti-Muslim Rhetoric from Far-Right Leaders Played 'Major Role' in Radicalization of Finsbury Park Attacker, Police Say, *Evening Standard*, 1 February 2018, www.standard.co.uk/news/crime/darren-osborne-guilty-antimuslim-rhetoric-from-farright-leaders-played-major-role-in-radicalisation-a3755991.html.

24 *Channel Four News*, Inside Facebook: Secrets of the Social Network, transmitted 17 July 2018; Figures such as Steve Bannon have given Yaxley-Lennon their backing. Sarah Marsh, Steve Bannon Says Tommy Robinson Should Be Released from Prison, *Guardian*, 15 July 2018, www.theguardian.com/us-news/2018/jul/15/steve-bannon-tommy-robinson-released-from-prison-trump-strategist-lbc-radio-interview; Andrew Gilligan, Tommy Robinson Is Best-Funded Politician in UK, *Sunday Times*, 10 March 2019, 14.

25 Alex Stamos Twitter Thread, 28 April 2019, https://twitter.com/alexstamos/status/1122324462953619457?s=11; on Facebook's and the Christchurch terrorist incident, see Kate Klonick, Inside the Team at Facebook That Dealt with the Christchurch Shooting, *New Yorker*, 25 April 2019, www.newyorker.com/news/news-desk/inside-the-team-at-facebook-that-dealt-with-the-christchurch-shooting.

26 Joseph Cox and Jason Koebler, Facebook Bans White Nationalism and White Separatism, *Motherboard*, 28 March 2019, https://motherboard.vice.com/en_us/article/nexpbx/facebook-bans-white-nationalism-and-white-separatism; Chris Sonderby, Update on New Zealand, *Facebook Newsroom*, 18 March 2019, https://newsroom.fb.com/news/2019/03/update-on-new-zealand/; on Margot James's comments, Author's notes, Oxford Media Convention, 18 March 2019; Sheryl Sandberg, By Working Together, We Can Win Against Hate, *Instagram-Press*, 29 March 2019, https://instagram-press.com/blog/2019/03/29/by-working-together-we-can-win-against-hate/; Rhys Blakely, Facebook 'Still Allowing the Broadcast of New Zealand Shooting, *The Times*, 3 April 2019, www.thetimes.co.uk/article/facebook-still-allowing-the-broadcast-of-christchurch-terror-attacks-7q99cxhsk; Standing Against Hate, *Facebook Newsroom*, 27 March 2019, https://newsroom.fb.com/news/2019/03/standing-against-hate/; Bryan Menegus, Here's 40 Pages of Facebook Trying to Figure Out What to Do About White Nationalism, *Gizmodo*, 8 April 2019, https://gizmodo.com/heres-40-pages-of-facebook-trying-to-figure-out-what-to-1833888450; Louise Casey and Mark Rowley, Our Efforts to Stop Extremism Are Undermined at Every Turn, *Sunday Times*, 17 March 2019, www.thetimes.co.uk/article/our-efforts-to-stop-extremism-are-undermined-at-every-turn-cwwrm3d3t; Jonathan Albright, Hate Almost-Crimes and the Rise of Inter-Nationalism, *Medium*, 8 April 2019, https://medium.com/@d1gi/hate-almost-crimes-and-the-rise-of-inter-nationalism-45fb0a752adb; Alex Hern, Facebook Bans Far-Right Groups Including BNP, EDL and Britain First, *Guardian*, 18 April 2019, www.theguardian.com/technology/2019/apr/18/facebook-bans-far-right-groups-including-bnp-edl-and-britain-first; House of Commons, 2019c. Lizzie Dearden, Neo-Nazi Groups Allowed to Stay on Facebook Because They 'Do Not Violate Community Standards', *Independent*, 24 March 2019, www.independent.co.uk/news/uk/home-news/facebook-new-zealand-neo-nazis-white-supremacists-a8837886.html?utm_source=reddit.com and Andy Campbell, Facebook Says White Nationalist Video Doesn't Break New Policy Against White Nationalism, *HuffPost US*, 3 April 2019, www.huffingtonpost.ca/

entry/facebook-white-nationalism-faith-goldy-video_n_5ca37bade4b0f2df86
69c196.

27 Leo Mirani, Millions of Facebook Users Have No Idea They're Using the Internet,
    Quartz, 9 February 2015, https://qz.com/333313/milliions-of-facebook-users-
    have-no-idea-theyre-using-the-internet/.

28 Amanda Taub and Max Fischer, Where Countries Are a Tinderbox and
    Facebook Is a Match, *New York Times*, 21 April 2018, www.nytimes.com/
    2018/04/21/world/asia/facebook-sri-lanka-riots.html.

29 Ryan Mac, Charlie Warzel and Alex Kantrowicz, Growth at Any Cost: Top
    Facebook Executive Defended Data Collection in 2016 Memo – and Warned
    That Facebook Could Get People Killed, *Buzzfeed*, 29 March 2018, www.
    buzzfeednews.com/article/ryanmac/growth-at-any-cost-top-facebook-execu
    tive-defended-data, United Nations Human Rights Council, Report of the
    Independent International Fact-Finding Mission on Myanmar (A/HRC/39/64),
    27 August 2018, https://reliefweb.int/report/myanmar/report-independent-
    international-fact-finding-mission-myanmar-ahrc3964-advance; Nick Cohen, We
    Can't Halt the Spread of Hate If We Don't Get Tough with the Tech Giants,
    Observer, 30 September 2018, 50. Francis Wheen, Fleas We Greatly Loathe,
    London Review of Books, 5 July 2018, 23–26.

30 Steve Stecklow, Hatebook – Inside Facebook's Myanmar Operation, Special
    Report, *Reuters*, 15 August 2018, www.reuters.com/investigates/special-report/
    myanmar-facebook-hate/?utm_source=Sailthru&utm_medium=email&utm_
    campaign=Daily%20Intelligencer%20-%20August%2018%2C%202018%20-
    %20Campaign%201&utm_term=WR%20Test%208%2018%202018; Hadas
    Gold, Facebook Bans Myanmar Military Chief and Says It Was 'Too Slow' to Act,
    CNN, 27 August 2018, https://money.cnn.com/2018/08/27/technology/myan
    mar-army-facebook/index.html?utm_source=Daily+Lab+email+list&utm_
    campaign=cda91ce1a2-dailylabemail3&utm_medium=email&utm_term=0_
    d68264fd5e-cda91ce1a2-396076061.

31 Alex Warofka, An Independent Assessment of the Human Rights Impact
    of Facebook in Myanmar, *Facebook Newsroom*, 5 November 2018, https://
    newsroom.fb.com/news/2018/11/myanmar-hria/; BSR, Human Rights Impact
    Assessment: Facebook in Myanmar, October 2018, https://fbnewsroomus.files.
    wordpress.com/2018/11/bsr-facebook-myanmar-hria_final.pdf. Myanmar is not
    alone: demagogic leaders in other countries, such as Duterte in the Philippines,
    have also exploited Facebook ruthlessly (Vaidhyanathan, 190–193).

32 BBC, 2018 a and b; Rishi Iyengar, WhatsApp Has Been Linked to Lynchings in
    India: Facebook Has Been Trying to Contain the Crisis, 27 July 2018, https://
    money.cnn.com/2018/07/27/technology/facebook-whatsapp-india-misinforma
    tion/index.html?iid=EL; Antonio Garcia Martinez, Why WhatsApp Became a
    Hotbed for Rumors and Lies in Brazil, *Wired*, 4 November 2018, www.wired.
    com/story/why-whatsapp-became-a-hotbed-for-rumors-and-lies-in-brazil/;
    Matheus Magnanta, Juliana Gragnani and Felipe Souza, How WhatsApp
    Is Being Abused in Brazil's Elections, *BBC News Brasil*, 24 October 2018,
    www.bbc.co.uk/news/technology-45956557; Kartsten Schmehl, WhatsApp
    Has Become a Hotbed for Spreading Nazi Propaganda in Germany, *Buzzfeed*,
    18 April 2019, www.buzzfeednews.com/article/karstenschmehl/whatsapp-
    groups-nazi-symbol-stickers-germany; reports from India in the lead up to its
    2019 election suggested problems remain: Newley Purnell, Fake News Runs
    Wild on WhatsApp as India Elections Loom, *Wall Street Journal*, 31 March 2019,

www.wsj.com/articles/fake-news-is-rampant-on-whatsapp-as-indian-elections-loom-11554055428; Vindu Goel and Sheera Frenkel, In India False Posts and Hate Speech Flummox Facebook, *New York Times*, 1 April 2019, www.nytimes.com/2019/04/01/technology/india-elections-facebook.html.

33 Monika Bickert and Brian Fishman, Hard Questions: How We Counter Terrorism, *Facebook Newsroom*, 15 June 2017, https://newsroom.fb.com/news/2017/06/how-we-counter-terrorism/.

34 Edward Lucas, Why Rudd Is Wrong About Online Encryption, *The Times*, 4 August 2017, www.thetimes.co.uk/article/why-rudd-is-wrong-about-online-encryption-qrcnfhvh9; John Naughton, Facebook's New Encrypted Network Will Give Criminals the Privacy They Crave, *Observer*, New Review, 17 March 2019, 29; Ben Thompson, Facebook's Privacy Cake, *Stratechery*, 7 March 2019, https://stratechery.com/2019/facebooks-privacy-cake/; Comey, 2018.

7 Regulating Facebook's dominance

Done is better than Perfect.
  – Sign painted on Facebook walls at the time of its 2012 IPO[1]

Facebook is under regulatory and political scrutiny around the world. A significant range of regulatory proposals has been advanced to address the kinds of challenges identified in this book. These include anti-trust and competition policy matters; regulation of the digital advertising systems that support Facebook and others, including programmatic advertising; changes to electoral laws to reflect the realities of digital advertising; further requirements to govern take-down of hate speech, terrorist-supporting material, child pornography and other material in some cases, including disinformation or fake news, supported by fines; and action to make Facebook pay a greater share of taxation.

Belatedly, Facebook has become a convert to further regulation. Mark Zuckerberg posted ideas for regulation on his Facebook page and in the *Washington Post* in March 2019. He said there were four key areas: harmful content; fair elections; harmonised data and privacy regulation, along the lines of Europe's GDPR; and 'true' data portability, which would allow users to switch their data to another platform. Research by the Harvard academic Debora L. Spar suggests we shouldn't be surprised by this. During most waves of technological development, it is often the incumbents who are the first to call for it. Within weeks, Facebook lobbyists were telling Congress Zuckerberg's comments were for international consumption, but in June, congressional hearings began.[2]

Zuckerberg told Congress that smaller incumbents may suffer more, as they will not have the resources to deal with regulation in the way that larger companies such as Facebook do. On the contrary, it is possible to develop a graded approach which deals with the most dominant operators, as the UK White Paper published in April 2019 suggests. This could be further strengthened by adding specific rules around company turnover or number of users or percentage of users in Facebook's market on a daily or monthly basis, as the German Competition Authority, the Bundeskartellamt, identifies in its February 2019 judgement.[3]

Regulators and government have been developing their discursive capacity around these issues, with significant input from academics and intellectuals. We should think of regulation as a process, not an event. There is a cycle ranging from problem-identification in the public arena, which can itself lead to corrective action, through a variety of regulatory and governance proposals and their adoption and enforcement by regulators or the courts. Corrective action sometimes happens in the market-place – Apple has taken regulatory action against Facebook, kicking some of its apps off its platform,[4] and advertiser boycotts have happened.

Regulatory proposals range from reliance on the general law, public pressure, agreed industry collective norms of self-regulation by trade bodies, co-regulation involving co-operation by companies and state bodies and regulation set down in and underpinned by statute.

Facebook's scale and dominance are factors driving regulatory action. Martin Moore and Damian Tambini state that digital platforms not only operate on a scale bigger than previous regulatory challenges, giving them structural dominance, but also have explicit political and social aims and perform genuine civic functions. Tarleton Gillespie says that social media platforms are neither conduit nor content, nor are they just network or media, but a hybrid not previously anticipated in regulation: 'a fundamentally new information configuration, materially, institutionally, financially, and socially'.[5]

Facebook of course is already subject to regulation. It is regulated by the Securities and Exchange Commission (SEC) in respect of its reporting to shareholders, and the SEC has been investigating it over the Cambridge Analytica issue, as have the US Department of Justice securities fraud division, the FBI and the FTC. Facebook told investors in April 2019 it was preparing for an FTC fine of potentially $3–5 billion. Thirty-eight state attorneys in the US are investigating Facebook. Meanwhile, Facebook benefits from regulation every day. As Cass Sunstein says, so do its users:

> If you have a Facebook account, you didn't pay for it. But it's definitely yours.[6]

The new challenge to Facebook's power comes principally from two areas: the resurrection of anti-trust and competition concerns and the intersection of data protection policy and competition policy, which is under active discussion both at academic and institutional levels and in consumer lobbying in the EU and publisher lobbying globally.[7] Institutionally, the IMF, the OECD, the European Competition Commissioner, the FTC, the Australian Competition and Consumer Commission, the German Bundeskartellamt, the UK House of Lords and House of Commons, the Cairncross Review and the Furman Review for the UK Treasury have all raised these issues.[8]

Facebook is subject to data protection laws in countries which have them, to competition law and to a variety of other laws governing unlawful content. In respect of data issues, it has been fined by the European Competition Commissioner and the UK Information Commissioner. In May 2018, the European Union's General Data Protection Regulation (GDPR) came into force, placing new responsibilities on data controllers and new levels of fines that could be imposed of up to 4% of global annual turnover. In evidence to the US Senate, prior to its implementation, Mark Zuckerberg suggested that he might be willing to consider the GDPR as a gold standard for data regulation for Facebook globally, though he was to row back from that position subsequently. Facebook frequently lobbies against the tightening of rules on its activities, from the 2011 Federal Election Commission attempts to tighten of laws on digital election advertising, to GDPR, which Zuckerberg admitted may have cost Facebook one million users, to the 2018 California Consumer Privacy legislation. In April 2019, Facebook accepted changes in its Terms and Conditions which more clearly state how they use the data of their users for targeted advertising, following discussions with the European Commission and consumer authorities across Europe.[9]

Regulation, as Roger McNamee has said, is about changing a company's behavioural incentives. Following Germany's Network Enforcement Act (NetzDG) requiring speedy removal of illegal content, including hate speech, the bulk of Facebook moderators employed in Europe focus on Germany. This is a good example of what Ed Richards, the former chief executive of the UK communications regulator Ofcom, has called the 'nudge' power of regulation.[10]

The key driver behind the new regulatory approach is Facebook's dominance. Mark Zuckerberg has regularly referred to Facebook as 'a social utility' or simply, 'a utility', and in his manifesto in 2017, he referred to it as 'social infrastructure' on several occasions. Utilities, of course, are regulated – and so is critical infrastructure. The potential for exploitation by hostile state actors certainly means that Facebook is now critical social infrastructure.

A growing number of organisations and individuals are now suggesting that Facebook should be treated as a utility or as critical social infrastructure. Researchers in the US have sought to re-examine and revive the public utility concept to address 'concentrated private power'. The House of Lords Communications Committee (2019) drew on evidence from this author, which suggested that Big Tech companies should be designated as information utilities and concluded that it was appropriate to put special obligations on companies such as Facebook to ensure that they acted fairly to users, to other companies 'and in the interests of society'. These obligations would be enforced by a regulator. Hindman suggests they should be seen as 'attention utilities' providing critical distribution infrastructure which cannot be substituted. Senator Elizabeth Warren has called for regulation of what she calls the 'Platform Utilities':

> Companies with an annual global revenue of $25 billion or more and that offer to the public an online marketplace, an exchange, or a platform for connecting third parties would be designated as 'platform utilities.'
>
> These companies would be prohibited from owning both the platform utility and any participants on that platform. Platform utilities would be required to meet a standard of fair, reasonable, and non-discriminatory dealing with users. Platform utilities would not be allowed to transfer or share data with third parties.

Senator Mark Warner has proposed a revision of 'essential facilities determinations' to ensure that beyond a certain threshold 'user base size, market share, or level of dependence of wider ecosystems' certain platforms would be recognised as critical infrastructure. Although ideas like this have been considered occasionally over recent years and pushed hard by organisations like the Open Markets Institute, there are now signs that these ideas are being given credence on all sides of the political debate, although the libertarian lobby against this remains strong. Facebook's latest move, Zuckerberg's pivot to privacy, designed to integrate Facebook, WhatsApp and Instagram, if it makes break-up harder, may require utility treatment as the default.[11]

We need an overall framework to address dominance because an approach based simply on rectification of harms and providing redress for individual issues is unlikely to capture the systematic nature of the problems thrown up by dominant players whose very business model provides financial incentives for abuse. The starting point has to be to put the Big Tech companies on a clear statutory footing in national and supra-national laws on digital market competition. There are precedents from telecommunications and broadcasting regulation, where specific categories of companies have been defined, and controls on their abilities to dominate markets established. Taking the UK as an example, British Telecom, after privatisation in 1984, was prohibited for many years from entering the television market until effective competition had been established. From 1990, independent television companies, and the BBC, were required to have a significant percentage of their programmes made by independent television producers.

Merger legislation could also be amended: in the UK, the CMA currently uses three public interest categories for mergers: media plurality, national security and financial stability. Its chief executive told the House of Lords Communications Committee in 2018 that Parliament could add a fourth category, such as 'the creation of data monopolies'. Had that existed in 2012, it might have forced a more detailed examination of the Facebook/Instagram merger. It doesn't however tell us what to do now.[12]

Former Ofcom regulator Robin Foster argued in 2012 that in respect of any new regulatory framework, 'there are advantages in having some form of statutory underpinning, to secure public trust and clear and independent accountability'. New legislation could be introduced, establishing a framework by which these dominant data monopolies might be categorised (in each of social, search, news aggregation and distribution and digital store categories, previously identified by Foster, and the addition perhaps of another category of advertising platform). Tests of dominance would be triggered, as I have suggested earlier. Following the triggering of those tests, a consultation might be undertaken by the relevant regulator (or regulators, as it is possible that the interests of a number of regulators might be engaged). Depending on the outcome of that consultation, it would be a matter for the relevant secretary of state to determine that a specific company would be categorised as an information utility (there would be nothing to stop the foundational legislation determining that certain companies were automatically to be considered information utilities). Information utilities would be licensed as such, and they would have specific reporting regulations in respect of the designated regulator, which would be granted strong back-stop intervention powers. Dominant information utilities would have the most stringent reporting duties, which would be based on far greater transparency around their operations.

The way into this discussion may be through consideration of the information utilities' role in online advertising, where the duopoly dominates. Attacking advertising concentration attacks Facebook's power, as we can see from the ACCC examination in Australia. The ACCC found that both Facebook and Google had 'substantial market power' in certain markets. It is estimated that 68% of advertising spending is going to them. They need particular scrutiny, because the dominant businesses are vertically integrated, that is, present at multiple levels of the same supply chain. Facebook is vertically integrated through the Facebook audience network and the services offered on Facebook platforms.

The ACCC has found that there is a lack of transparency which means that 'advertisers do not know what they are paying for, where their

advertisements are being displayed, and to whom'. Transparency on metrics is an issue, as we have already seen, as is ad fraud, and the opacity
around programmatic advertising means that advertisers don't know if they
are getting value for money. As different regulatory conditions apply to
digital platforms from media companies, the ACCC says there is a 'regulatory imbalance' which may provide an unfair advantage to platforms 'in
attracting advertising expenditure'. The ACCC said there may be merit
in a regulator monitoring the digital advertising market in respect of the
behaviours of dominant players and the pricing of digital advertising.[13] It
was the lack of transparency which made the case for a competition inquiry
into online advertising in the UK, said both Cairncross and Furman. Meanwhile, a US FTC commissioner has suggested that behavioural advertising
technologies

> radically alter the relationship between platform, user, and content.
> Under the behavioural advertising model, companies don't place ads
> by targeting content; they place ads by targeting people.

The German Cartel Authority, the Bundeskartellamt, has called Facebook's
combination of data on individual users, drawn from a variety of data
sources, 'an exploitative abuse' of its dominant position. If its judgement is
confirmed, Facebook's advertising model, based on the massive accumulation of data which makes it so attractive to advertisers, will be called into
question, unless it gets direct consent from users. The e-Privacy directive
could also have a significant impact on Facebook and Google, according
to the US publishers' association, Digital Content Next, and their ability to
harvest data.[14] The UK's Information Commissioner has also begun serious work on advertising technology, with research indicating how little it
is understood by users and how more understanding of its nature results in
greater concern about it.[15]

It is sometimes argued that the most effective way to regulate Facebook
would be some form of structural separation – to break it up, stripping it of
WhatsApp and Instagram or Facebook Messenger. Siva Vaidhyanathan says
that Facebook, WhatsApp, Instagram, Oculus Rift and Facebook Messenger
should be severed from 'the core Facebook application and company', and
each should compete against each other. However, some legal scholars like
Harold Feld warn of the 'starfish problem':

> 'If you tear up a starfish, the pieces regrow and instead of one starfish
> you have five starfish,' says Feld. 'If you're going to split up Facebook,
> what's to prevent it becoming three Facebooks, each one dominant in its
> particular market segment?'[16]

Arguably, the real power centre of Facebook is its vertical integration as a social media network, a media distribution company, a media buying company, an advertising exchange or platform, an advertising agency and a data analytics company; its horizontally integrated data exchanges between Facebook, WhatsApp, Messenger and Instagram; and the ability of advertisers to sell across the Facebook companies. Structural separation of these functions might be a powerful solution. Damian Tambini has suggested separating Facebook's advertising and editorial functions (e.g., in the News Feed). Channel Four in the UK was originally prohibited from selling its own advertising. It would be entirely possible for regulators to take action to restrict Facebook's freedom of manoeuvre in a number of these areas, preventing it from operating its own advertising exchange, preventing the cross-company sharing of data or cross-selling of advertising and forcing its advertising operation to operate as an external buyer against competitive operations also granted access in a form of regulated unbundling and no doubt in other ways. These are all challenges which one might expect an empowered regulator to examine.

Academic commentators and legislative inquiries have looked at structures of regulation. Different jurisdictions have different lead regulators for digital industries. Key to their effectiveness are a clear remit for oversight, the necessary technical expertise and strong enforcement powers and staffing. In many cases, there needs to be close and effective cooperation between different regulators in the competition, data, media and telecommunications regulation, algorithmic governance and election regulation fields, with regulators empowered to share information and work collaboratively, between them and regulators in other nation-states. A standing authority to identify emerging gaps in regulation and to fill them would also be useful, as the House of Lords recently suggested, identifying the need for a Digital Authority to instruct and coordinate other regulators.[17]

Aside from a regulatory framework to address questions of dominance, there are sector-specific issues which need to be addressed and which have been examined by a number of researchers. These include media plurality; electoral law; policies for moderation and take-down of abusive posts, hate-speech, terrorist and extremist content; advertising regulation; data, including issues where data ownership affects competition; and algorithmic accountability. Taxation to address value extraction and levies to support quality media also need to be addressed.

Proposals to address platform impact on media plurality have been advanced by a number of authors. These proposals are intended to address both plurality issues affecting the media industry as a whole and the experience of the users themselves in terms of enabling their exposure to a diverse range of sources (exposure diversity). Proposals for media plurality include adopting the 'due prominence' approach set down in, for example, the EU's Access Directive, to ensure fair, reasonable and non-discriminatory access for media organisations to the platforms through which individuals increasingly consume their media, including the possibility of requiring 'must-carry' provisions (i.e., that the platforms 'must carry' certain kinds of content, e.g., public service broadcasting), backstop regulation in respect of access guarantees and cross-media ownership restrictions, effective remedies and codes of practice in respect of content in each domain of intermediary activity.

A number of researchers and organisations have stressed the need to update laws on elections and regulations, and in a number of these areas, Facebook has decided to change its own rules. Proposals have included suspending micro-targeting of political advertising; aligning rules on television and online advertising; ensuring that online materials produced by parties, candidates and campaigners reveal their source and funding; stronger internal procedures to check eligibility of spending and ensure that it is monitored; tightening of rules to prevent foreign donations being used in elections and referendums, including by subsidiary companies of foreign-controlled companies; online databases of political adverts; fair pricing of campaign advertising for all candidates, rather than leaving it to the automated advertising exchanges of social media platforms; stronger investigatory powers for election regulators to obtain information and the ability to impose tougher sanctions; and commitments to ethical messaging and greater transparency and accountability by political parties for the data that they have collected on voters and processed. France has passed a law specifying that candidates in elections can ask judges to order the removal of fake news which is being circulated and including rules on transparency of social media advertising.[18]

It is in the area of platform liability that the legacy legislation of the Internet era comes under challenge. The legacy legislation includes of course Section 230 of the US Communications Decency Act of 1996, the EU's E-Commerce Directive of 2000 and the UK's 2003 Communications Act.[19] The first two limited the liability of Internet platforms as carriers of information akin to USPs. The UK legislation created Ofcom without a remit for regulation of the Internet. The principles underlying S230 and the E-Commerce directive are now under challenge in jurisdictions around the world.

Unlawful speech, including conspiracy, bribery and child pornography, has always been regulated, as Cass Sunstein says, even in the United States, even under the First Amendment to the Constitution. Gillespie says there have always been measures to address abusive hate speech or obscenity, often operated as self-regulatory systems by the early ISPs, such as CompuServe. The First Amendment is designed to prevent Congress passing laws that prevent free speech, not to ensure that everyone has a right to have their views carried on major platforms. Ben Wagner argues, however, that one of the issues raised by Facebook's global operations is that it seeks in effect to promote American speech norms across the world. Pragmatically, it has been forced to address different legislative approaches in delivering its services to countries beyond the United States, which may have – for example Germany – stronger rules on the regulation of hate speech.[20]

In 2016, the European Union secured agreement from Big Tech companies to a code of conduct on hate speech and takedown and issued a Communication on these issues in 2017, laying down guidelines and principles for platforms. Countries around the world, including Australia, India and Singapore, have developed new measures around the takedown of illegal content or disinformation. I don't argue that these laws are perfect, unproblematic or uncontested: as with the UK proposals announced in April 2019, many questions remain, including around due process, precision in definition of prohibited material and satisfaction of human rights principles.[21]

Facebook dominance drives the reforms, along with a growing distrust of Facebook's seriousness about these issues, no matter the avowed commitment of its senior figures. Facebook now commands little confidence, because it has been found wanting before and because its decisions on content moderation have appeared inconsistent, contradictory, capricious and compromised by the profit motive. Legislative and regulatory frustration with Facebook and other platforms has turned to the question of criminal penalties on the senior managements of platform companies. The new Australian law on social media violent content suggests fines of up to 10% of annual revenue and up to three years in prison for executives found to have offended. The recent UK White Paper on Internet Safety suggests fines amounting to 4% of annual turnover; as with GDPR, the new online safety regulator will have the power 'to disrupt the business activities of a non-compliant company', as well as the ability to target individual managers with fines. An FTC commissioner suggested that there might need to be prison time for repeat offenders or personal fines or obligations, bonus crackdowns, bans on business practices and closing of business lines.[22]

Journalists and lawmakers regularly complain at Facebook's failure to act swiftly to remove content that not only breaks its terms of service and community guidelines but also frequently breaks the law. Facebook has created teams of moderators, sometimes in-house, often sub-contracted. Its guidelines to these moderators were leaked to the UK's *Guardian* newspaper in 2017 and were revealed to be 'a messy and disturbing hodgepodge', in the words of the researcher Tarleton Gillespie, who has studied social media moderation in detail.[23]

Facebook responds by pointing to the amount of material posted on its platform every day, with billions of posts and hundreds of millions of photographs. It has to moderate at 'industrial scale' as Robyn Caplan says. Others argue that Facebook is effectively being subsidised for the costs of its own failures by users, media organisations and others who flag up problem materials. Instead, it should be investing sufficiently to address the online pollution that it is causing, under the 'polluter pays' principle that underpins much environmental legislation. More serious is Facebook's failure to implement the promises that it has made: it seems repeatedly to be caught out. In November 2018, the *Intercept* news organisation was able to select 'white' as a category of advertising, a year after *ProPublica* had been able to use the category 'Jew hater' and Facebook had promised to clean up its act, signing an agreement with the Attorney General of Washington State. But now it faces a lawsuit from the US Department of Housing and Urban Development for allegedly violating the Fair Housing Act by allowing advertisers to exclude certain races, religions or genders.[24]

Facebook has announced plans to double from 10,000 to 20,000 the number of individuals worldwide employed in content moderation. Stories have regularly surfaced about the pressures on Facebook content moderators in terms of both their daily targets for appraising contents and the impact on their mental health of the vile content that they have to police. The rules are also enforced inconsistently, with far-right activists kept on Facebook for years even after rule breaches or holocaust denial posts kept up even in jurisdictions where they are illegal. The House of Lords Communications Committee heard evidence in 2018 from Matt Reynolds, a journalist with *WIRED UK*, who had reported far-right content to Facebook 'that had a reach of millions of people in the UK'. Initially, Facebook took no action. He then found that Facebook had taken it down, but he found it 'very hard' to get clarity from Facebook about why the decision had been made.[25]

Gillespie points out that Facebook's decision to change the News Feed from a chronologically curated flow of information to an algorithmically chosen selection was profitable for the platform but says that shift makes Facebook more liable for the content that is made available. This act of algorithmic sorting is said to be what differentiates platforms from mere carriers of content and is now being raised by regulators as a reason for amending their liability obligations under S230 in the US. This is a highly contested area of policy at both a practical and a theoretical level.[26]

Doubts are also raised about the effectiveness and independence of Facebook's internal structures. Facebook has advisory boards. How free are the members? Are they muzzled by non-disclosure agreements? What is the financial connection, if any, between Facebook and the individuals who sit on them? These are questions that are legitimate for regulators – and lawmakers – to ask. This applies to Facebook's proposed Oversight Board for Content Decisions, announced by new Facebook vice-president of Global Affairs and Communications, former UK Deputy Prime Minister Nick Clegg. Membership will be chosen by Facebook.[27] Based on his observations of Facebook's Safety Advisory Board, respected Internet safety adviser, John Carr, is sceptical. He, like others, has long advocated the notion of a 'duty of care' now proposed in the UK Internet Safety White Paper.

Wagner suggests minimum standards of content moderation stipulated under legislation. If there is to be confidence in Facebook's internal processes, regulators will need to be reassured that there is due process in place, that Facebook isn't adjusting its rules to suit itself, for example when repeat violators are allowed to keep posting if they have large groups of followers who keep engaging with their material and raising revenue for Facebook. There will also need to be proper internal whistle-blowing procedures for staff who identify that Facebook practices are likely to cause breaches of rules. It is likely that we are heading to a form of 'statutory underpinning' of Facebook's practices, with firm codes of practice agreed with regulators – regulated self-regulation, in other words, with codes of practice which draw on the Santa Clara principles on transparency and accountability in content moderation or the Manila Principles, based on international human rights law. Issues of child abuse and terrorism are already the subject of specific laws in most territories, and there is evidence from law enforcement agencies of effective co-operation – but even here, doubts have been raised about Facebook's internal practices, particularly in relation to Instagram,[28] and as we have seen, the Christchurch terrorist incident has called into question the basic operation of the Facebook Live service without more effective controls.

Other areas where Facebook faces challenges over moderation of content and takedown lie in consumer protection policy – for example, anti-vaccination advertising and propaganda, influencer advertising, dishonest advertising – and in copyright. Where the law is clear, then the responsibility lies with Facebook to implement instructions determined in law, by courts or advertising regulators, and they can be held to account for a failure to address those issues. The general problem lies more in public trust in Facebook's ability or willingness to implement its own policies.

Algorithmic governance and regulation has become an intense area of debate.[29] The UK White Paper also addresses concerns around the algorithms used by social media companies such as Facebook and the need for regulators to have more insight as to how these operate. This includes the right to demand explanations of how they make the distribution of disinformation more likely and how they organise and select content aimed at children and a power to inspect them in situ to assess for bias or other ethical issues, including designed addiction.

In the past, EU action against the major platforms was attacked, including by President Obama, as protectionist. Antitrust specialist Lina Khan has said that is 'just insulting'.[30] But platform liability is a trade issue for the United States, with the United States Trade Representative recently saluting the new trade agreement with Canada and Mexico, which includes a clause to

> Limit the civil liability of Internet platforms for third-party content that such platforms host or process, outside of the realm of intellectual property enforcement, thereby enhancing the economic viability of these engines of growth that depend on user interaction and user content.

Libertarian lobbies, such as the American Enterprise Institute, have said that the EU's GDPR represents trade tariffs by other means, and data deals should be incorporated in trade talks. In contrast, the EU and Japan have allowed data to flow unimpeded between the two economies, as Japan's rules were deemed the equivalent of Europe's.[31]

Franklin Foer says that Big Tech companies owe their dominance not only to innovation but also to 'tax avoidance'. Facebook will find itself subject to new kinds of digital taxes. In his October 2018 budget, the UK Chancellor of the Exchequer, Philip Hammond, announced a new Digital Services Tax, which would be levied on the revenues of the 'Big Tech' companies from 2020. This followed speculation over some months that an EU-wide tax would be imposed to prevent companies using tax arbitrage to ensure that they were taxed in the lowest possible tax jurisdictions and using complicated mechanisms of internal re-charging to re-state their profits in EU member states and in discussions within the OECD at G20 level. It seems likely that the full range of taxation measures has yet to be deployed. Legal scholar Lilian Edwards proposed a 'privacy tax' before Facebook was available to the general public, but these ideas are now being resurrected. Some have called for remedial taxes to address the impact of platforms on high street traders, on media companies and others; elsewhere, I have called for a connectivity tax to address cybersecurity concerns about the Internet of Things. A number of groups have suggested levies on the advertising revenues of companies such as Facebook and Google. Like so many other issues, political debate on these issues is emergent rather than conclusive. Taxation is one way to address the negative externalities of platforms such as Facebook or to fund social goods such as independent news.[32]

At the core of this discussion of course is corporate power in the age of surveillance capitalism. The evidence, increasingly, is that governments will not accept the status quo. Where Facebook has users, governments will regulate.

Notes

1 From Mark Zuckerberg's letter to investors, included in Facebook's 2012 IPO filing with the SEC, www.sec.gov/Archives/edgar/data/1326801/0001193125 12034517/d287954ds1.htm#toc287954_10.
2 Mark Zuckerberg, The Internet Needs New Rules: Let's Start in These Four Areas, *Washington Post*, 30 March 2019, www.washingtonpost.com/opinions/ mark-zuckerberg-the-internet-needs-new-rules-lets-start-in-these-four-areas/ 2019/03/29/9e6f0504-521a-11e9-a3f7-78b7525a8d5f_story.html?utm_ term=.42196eb6a00b and www.facebook.com/zuck/posts/10107013839885441; Spar (2001: 381–382); Cecilia Kang, It's US vs. World as Big Tech Faces Spectre of Limiting Speech Online, *New York Times*, 21 April 2019, https:// flipboard.com/@newyorktimes/free-speech-puts-u.s.-on-%E2%80%98a-col lision-course%E2%80%99-with-global-limits-on-big-tech/a-HYQm5q0NQT-HusuVrS6aTQ%3Aa%3A3195393-cbab1f0d61/nytimes.com; Emma Woolla-cott, Anti-Trust Probe Starts Today with Focus on Big Tech's Profits from News, *Forbes*, 11 June 2019, www.forbes.com/sites/emmawoollacott/2019/06/11/anti trust-probe-starts-today-with-focus-on-big-techs-profits-from-news/#5d0d409 f458a.
3 See Zuckerberg's comments before Congress, *Washington Post* 2018 a and b.
4 Mulligan and Griffin, 2018; Danny Fortson, Apple Boss Hits Out at Facebook Over Privacy, 3 February 2019, www.thetimes.co.uk/article/apple-boss-tim-cook-hits-out-at-facebook-over-privacy-grmmvp65w.
5 Moore and Tambini, 2018: 4; Gillespie, 2018: 41, 207.
6 Georgia Wells, SEC, FBI Question Facebook Over User Data, *Wall Street Journal*, 2 July 2018, www.wsj.com/articles/sec-fbi-question-facebook-over-user-data-1530575905; Dave Michaels and Georgia Wells, SEC Probes Why Facebook Didn't Warn Sooner on Privacy Lapse, *Wall Street Journal*, 12 July 2018, www.wsj.com/articles/sec-probes-why-facebook-didnt-warn-sooner-on-privacy-lapse-1531422043; Louise Matsakis, The FTC Is Officially Investigat-ing Facebook's Data Practices, *Wired*, 26 March 2018, www.wired.com/story/ ftc-facebook-data-privacy-investigation/; Facebook, 2019b. For the 38 US Attorney Generals figure, see Carole Cadwalladr, This story is a lesson in insti-tutional failure . . . there have been virtually no consequences for those who broke the law, *Observer*, New Review, 17 March 2019, 10. Sunstein, 2017: 180.
7 Recently, there has been a focus on the intertwining of data and competition issues: see Stucke and Grunes, 2016; Helberger et al., 2017; Khan, 2018; Wu, 2018; Srinivasan, 2019; Bureau of European Union Consumers, Discussion paper: EU competition policy and digital economy, 22 August 2018, www.beuc.eu/press-media/news-events/discussion-paper-eu-competition-law-and-digital-economy; Letter to Google from Digital Content Next European Publishers Council, News Media Alliance and News Media Association, 30 April 2018, www.news mediauk.org/write/MediaUploads/PDF%20Docs/DCN_Letter_to_Google_re_ GDPR_Terms.pdf; Paresh Dave, Publishers Rebuke Google's Interpretation of EU Privacy Law, *Reuters*, 30 April 2018, www.reuters.com/article/us-alphabet-privacy-publishers-gdpr/publishers-rebuke-googles-interpretation-of-eu-pri vacy-law-idUSKBN1I11GG.
8 EU Competition Commissioner Vestager has opened up discussions on com-petition policy in the digital age, which may result in tightened data portability options within GDPR and sector-specific regulation: EC, 2019. Similarly, in the

United States, the FTC held a series of hearings on the intersection between privacy, big data and competition and launched a Task Force to monitor competition issues in technology markets. www.ftc.gov/news-events/press-releases/2018/06/ftc-announces-hearings-competition-consumer-protection-21st www.ftc.gov/news-events/audio-video/2018-workshops https://stratechery.com/2018/netflixs-earnings-netflixs-marketing-choice-additional-notes-on-netflix/ and FTC's Bureau of Competition Launches Task Force to Monitor Technology Markets, 26 February 2019, www.ftc.gov/news-events/press-releases/2019/02/ftcs-bureau-competition-launches-task-force-monitor-technology.

9 Carole Cadwalladr and Duncan Campbell, Revealed: Facebook's Global Lobbying Against Data Privacy Laws, *Observer*, 3 March 2019, www.theguardian.com/technology/2019/mar/02/facebook-global-lobbying-campaign-against-data-privacy-laws-investment; Sarah Frier and Bill Allison, Facebook Fought Rules That Could Have Exposed Fake Russian Ads, *Bloomberg*, 4 October 2017, www.bloomberg.com/news/articles/2017-10-04/facebook-fought-for-years-to-avoid-political-ad-disclosure-rules; ICYMI: Ashkan Soltani comments on Facebook, the Californian Consumer Privacy Act, Data Privacy in UK House of Commons Committee Hearing, *Californians for Consumer Privacy*, 29 November 2018, www.caprivacy.org/post/icymi-ashkan-soltani-comments-on-facebook-the-california-consumer-privacy-act-and-data-privacy-in-uk-house-of-commons-committee-hearing; Laura Kayali, Inside Facebook's Fight Against European Regulation, *Politico.Eu*, 23 January 2019, www.politico.eu/article/inside-story-facebook-fight-against-european-regulation/. For details of the EU fine, see European Commission, Mergers: Commission Fines Facebook €110 Million for Providing Misleading Information About WhatsApp Takeover, 18 May 2017, http://europa.eu/rapid/press-release_IP-17-1369_en.htm; for the ICO fine, ICO issues maximum £500,000 fine to Facebook for failing to protect users' personal information, ICO, 25 October 2018, https://ico.org.uk/about-the-ico/news-and-events/news-and-blogs/2018/10/facebook-issued-with-maximum-500-000-fine/. For impact of GDPR on Facebook, see Facebook Inc., Second Quarter Results 2018 Conference Call, 25 July 2018, https://s21.q4cdn.com/399680738/files/doc_financials/2018/Q2/Q218-earnings-call-transcript.pdf; European Commission, Facebook changes its terms and clarifies its use of data for consumers following discussions with the European Commission and consumer authorities, 9 April 2019, europa.eu/rapid/press-release_IP-19-2048_en.pdf.

10 Mcnamee, 2019: 113. For Ed Richards 'nudge' comment, see House of Lords Communications Committee, 'Exit' Interview with Ed Richards, 18 November 2014, www.parliament.uk/business/committees/committees-a-z/lords-select/communications-committee/publications/?type=&session=26&sort=false&inquiry=all.

11 On Zuckerberg and the utility concept, see Kirkpatrick, 2011, and Gillian Reagan, The Evolution of Facebook's Mission Statement, *Observer.com*, 13 July 2009, https://observer.com/2009/07/the-evolution-of-facebooks-mission-statement/; Zuckerberg, 2017, op cit; Rahman, 2018 a and b; House of Lords, 2019; Hindman, 2018: 171; Ryan Grim, Steve Bannon Wants Facebook and Google Regulated Like Utilities, *The Intercept*, 27 July 2017, https://theintercept.com/2017/07/27/steve-bannon-wants-facebook-and-google-regulated-like-utilities/; Senator Elizabeth Warren, Here's How We Can Break Up Big Tech, Team Warren, *Medium*, 8 March 2019, https://medium.com/@team

warren/heres-how-we-can-break-up-big-tech-9ad9e0da324c; White Paper (DRAFT) – US Sen. Mark R. Warner, Potential Policy Proposals for Regulation of Social Media and Technology Firms, 30 July 2018, www.ftc.gov/system/files/documents/public_comments/2018/08/ftc-2018-0048-d-0104-155263.pdf; Open Markets Institute, https://openmarketsinstitute.org/about-us/.

12 Office of Fair Trading Anticipated acquisition by Facebook Inc of Instagram Inc ME/5525/12, 22 August 2012, https://webarchive.nationalarchives.gov.uk/20140402232639/www.oft.gov.uk/shared_oft/mergers_ea02/2012/facebook.pdf.

13 Rod Sims, Examining the Impact of Digital Platforms on Competition in Media and Advertising Markets, 27 February 2019, www.accc.gov.au/speech/examining-the-impact-of-digital-platforms-on-competition-in-media-and-advertising-markets.

14 Prepared remarks of Federal Trade Commissioner Rohit Chopra, Tech Platforms, Content Creators, and Immunity, 28 March 2019, www.ftc.gov/public-statements/2019/03/prepared-remarks-commissioner-rohit-chopra-aba-tech-platforms-content; Emily Dreyfuss, German Regulators Just Outlawed Facebook's Entire Ad Business, *Wired*, 7 February 2019, www.wired.com/story/germany-facebook-antitrust-ruling/; Yvonne Cunnane and Nikhil Shanbhag, Why We Disagree with the Bundeskartellamt, *Facebook Newsroom*, 7 February 2019, https://newsroom.fb.com/news/2019/02/bundeskartellamt-order/. Jessica Davies, How EU's ePrivacy Law Could Affect Publishers, *Digiday*, 26 September 2017, https://digiday.com/media/guide-eus-eprivacy-regulation/.

15 Ben Thompson, Mark Zuckerberg's Proposal, the Copyright Directive and Sunk Costs, You Say You Want Some Regulation, *Stratechery*, 2 April 2019, https://stratechery.com/2019/mark-zuckerbergs-proposal-the-copyright-directive-and-sunk-costs-you-say-you-want-some-regulation/; ICO, Summary Report of Adtech Fact Finding Forum, 6 March 2019, https://ico.org.uk/about-the-ico/research-and-reports/adtech-fact-finding-forum/.

16 Vaidhyanathan, 2018: 216; Russell Brandom, The Monopoly-Busting Case Against Google, Amazon, Uber and Facebook, *The Verge*, 5 September 2018, www.theverge.com/2018/9/5/17805162/monopoly-antitrust-regulation-google-amazon-uber-facebook.

17 See, for example, Damian Tambini, How to 'Break Up' Facebook, *LSE Media Policy Blog*, 2 May 2018, http://blogs.lse.ac.uk/mediapolicyproject/2018/05/02/how-to-break-up-facebook/. Moore and Tambini, 2018; House of Lords, 2018; House of Commons, 2018; House of Lords, 2019; House of Commons, 2019.

18 Tambini, 2018; ICO, 2018a, b and c; Electoral Commission, 2018; Zachary Young, French Parliament Passes Law Against Fake News, *Politico*, 4 July 2018, www.politico.eu/article/french-parliament-passes-law-against-fake-news/; Jim Waterson, Inquiry Launched into Data Use from No-Deal Brexit Ads on Facebook, *Guardian*, 5 April 2019, www.theguardian.com/politics/2019/apr/04/inquiry-launched-into-data-use-from-no-deal-brexit-ads-on-facebook.

19 Kohl, 2012.

20 Sunstein, 2017: 183; Gillespie, 2018: 27; Wagner, 2018.

21 The EU Code of Conduct on Countering Illegal Hate-Speech Online, https://ec.europa.eu/info/policies/justice-and-fundamental-rights/combatting-discrimination/racism-and-xenophobia/countering-illegal-hate-speech-online_en; Paul Karp, *Guardian*, Australia passes social media law penalizing platforms for violent content, *Guardian*, 4 April 2019, www.theguardian.com/media/2019/

apr/04/australia-passes-social-media-law-penalising-platforms-for-violent-content; Megha Baree, India's New Rules to Govern Social Media Raise Fears of Even More Censorship, *Forbes*, 22 January 2019, www.forbes.com/sites/meghabahree/2019/01/22/indias-new-rules-to-govern-social-media-raise-fears-of-more-censorship/#79c3a1de6759; Saqib Shah, Singapore Plans to Pass Its Own Fake News Law, *Engadget*, 1 April 2019, www.engadget.com/2019/04/01/singapore-fake-news-law/.

22 Commissioner's Memorandum: Repeat Offenders 2018–01, *FTC*, 14 May 2018, www.ftc.gov/public-statements/2018/05/commissioners-memorandum-2018-01-repeat-offenders.

23 Gillespie, 2018: 111.

24 Caplan, 2018; Sam Biddle, 2018, Facebook Allows Advertisers to Target Users Interested in 'White Genocide', https://theintercept.com/2018/11/02/facebook-ads-white-supremacy-pittsburgh-shooting/; Julia Angwin, Madeline Varner and Ariana Tobin, 2017, www.propublica.org/article/facebook-enabled-advertisers-to-reach-jew-haters; AG Ferguson Investigation Leads to Facebook Making Nationwide Changes to Prohibit Discriminatory Advertisements on Its Platform, 24 July 2018, www.atg.wa.gov/news/news-releases/ag-ferguson-investigation-leads-facebook-making-nationwide-changes-prohibit; Adi Robertson, What Happens Next in the Housing Discrimination Case Against Facebook, *The Verge*, 2 April 2019, www.theverge.com/2019/4/2/18286660/facebook-hud-housing-discrimination-case-section-230-legal-defense.

25 Mark Bridge, Sick Facebook Videos Left Me Traumatised, Says Moderator, *The Times*, 6 October 2018, 35; Mark Bridge and Simon Duke, Facebook Staff Are Baffled by Its Censorship Rules, *The Times*, 29 December 2018, 12; John Naughton, That Facebook Is Broken Is Obvious from Its Burnt-Out Army of Moderators, *Observer New Review*, 6 January 2019, 13; Stephen Bleach, It's a Dirty, Damaging Job Trying to Clean Up the Internet, *Sunday Times, News Review*, 3 March 2019, 25; Nick Hopkins, Revealed: Facebook's Rulebook on Sex, Terrorism and Violence, *Guardian*, 21 May 2017, www.theguardian.com/news/2017/may/21/revealed-facebook-internal-rulebook-sex-terrorism-violence; Nick Hopkins, How Facebook Flouts Holocaust Denial Rules Except Where It Fears Being Sued, *Guardian*, 24 May 2017, www.theguardian.com/news/2017/may/24/how-facebook-flouts-holocaust-denial-laws-except-where-it-fears-being-sued; Jim Taylor, Facebook Moderator: I Had to Be Prepared to See Anything, *BBC News Online*, 8 February 2018, www.bbc.co.uk/news/technology-42920554; Nicholas Hellen, Tech Giant Slow to Delete Lucrative Posts of Far Right, *Sunday Times*, 15 July 2012, 2; *Channel Four News*, Inside Facebook: Secrets of the Social Network, transmitted 17 July 2018; Jason Koebler and Joseph Cox, The Impossible Job: Inside Facebook's Struggle to Moderate 2 Billion People, *Motherboard*, 23 August 2018, https://motherboard.vice.com/en_us/article/xwk9zd/how-facebook-content-moderation-works; The Cleaners by Moritz Riesewieck and Hans Block, *PBS*, www.pbs.org/independentlens/films/the-cleaners/; Alex Hern, Facebook Protects Far-Right Activists Even After Rule Breaches, *Guardian*, 17 July 2018, www.theguardian.com/technology/2018/jul/17/facebook-protects-far-right-activists-even-after-rule-breaches-dispatches-c4; Max Fisher, Inside Facebook's Secret Rulebook for Global Political Speech, *New York Times*, 27 December 2018, www.nytimes.com/2018/12/27/world/facebook-moderators.html;Casey Newton, The Trauma Floor, *The Verge*, 25 February 2019, www.theverge.com/2019/2/25/18229714/

cognizant-facebook-content-moderator-interviews-trauma-working-condi tions-arizona; Simon van Zuylen-Wood, 'Men Are Scum': Inside Facebook's War on Hate Speech, *Vanity Fair*, 26 February 2019, www.vanityfair.com/ news/2019/02/men-are-scum-inside-facebook-war-on-hate-speech.

26 Gillespie, 2018: 43.

27 Nick Clegg, Charting a Course for an Oversight Board for Content Decisions, *Facebook Newsroom*, 28 January 2019, https://newsroom.fb.com/news/2019/01/ oversight-board/.

28 Rosalind Urwin and Gabriel Pogrund, Instagram Staff 'Knew Site Could Be Used by Paedophiles', *The Times*, 24 February 2019, www.thetimes.co.uk/ article/instagram-staff-knew-site-could-be-used-by-paedophiles-bwm6hp5l7.

29 See, inter alia, House of Lords, 2018; Pasquale, 2015, Andrews, 2019.

30 Liz Gannes, Obama Says European Aggressiveness Towards Google Comes from Protecting Lesser Companies, *Recode*, 13 February 2015; Rana Foroohar: Lunch with the FT: Lina Khan, *Financial Times, Life and Arts*, 30–31 March 2019, 3.

31 Daniel Lyons, GDPR Privacy as Europe's Tariff by Other Means, *American Enterprise Institute*, 3 July 2018, www.aei.org/publication/gdpr-privacy-as-europes-tariff-by-other-means/; USTR, United States – Mexico- Canada Trade Factsheet – Modernising NAFTA into a 21st Century Trade Agreement, https:// ustr.gov/trade-agreements/free-trade-agreements/united-states-mexico-canada-agreement/fact-sheets/modernizing; Steve Lohr, AI and Privacy Concerns Get White House to Embrace Global Cooperation, *New York Times*, 3 April 2019, www.nytimes.com/2019/04/03/technology/artificial-intelligence-privacy-oecd.html.

32 Foer, 2018: 195; Edwards, 2004; Leighton Andrews, Algorithms, Governance and Regulation: Beyond the 'Necessary Hashtags', *LSE*, September 2017, www.lse.ac.uk/accounting/Assets/CARR/documents/D-P/Disspaper85.pdf; H.M. Treasury, *Digital Services Tax Consultation*, 7 November 2018, www. gov.uk/government/consultations/digital-services-tax-consultation; Ingrid Lunden, UK Chancellor Announces 2% 'Digital Services Tax' on Tech Giants' Revenues Starting in April 2020, *Techcrunch*, 29 October 2018, https://techcrunch. com/2018/10/29/uk-chancellor-announces-2-digital-services-tax-on-tech-giants-revenues-starting-in-april-2020/; Maïa de La Baume and Nicholas Vinocur, Macron Gives EU Tech Tax a Political Push, *Politico EU*, 23 October 2018, www.politico.eu/article/emmanuel-macron-eu-digital-tax-political-push/; OECD, *Addressing the Tax Challenges of the Digital Economy*, Paris: OECD, 2014, www.oecd-ilibrary.org/search?value1=digital+tax&option1=quicksearch& facetOptions=51&facetNames=pub_igoId_facet&operator51=AND&option51= pub_igoId_facet&value51=%27igo%2Foecd%27; Media Reform Coalition, Support New News Providers via a Levy on Digital Giants Like Google and Facebook, *Guardian*, 11 November 2016, www.theguardian.com/media/2016/nov/11/ protect-newspapers-via-a-levy-on-digital-giants-like-google-and-facebook.

Conclusion

Digital gangsters, morally bankrupt liars or just serial offenders?[1]

Since the Cambridge Analytica scandal burst into global prominence in March 2018, Facebook has been 'at war', according to its founder. The developments have seen the departure of many long-standing Facebook executives, including Facebook's respected chief security officer, Alex Stamos, and Chris Cox, tipped by *WIRED* to be Zuckerberg's successor, publicised tensions between Mark Zuckerberg and his chief operating officer Sheryl Sandberg, and questioning of Facebook's aggressive PR campaign against critics like George Soros. By the end of 2018, the founders of both WhatsApp and Instagram had left the company. WhatsApp's Jan Koum quit in the aftermath of the Cambridge Analytica scandal, allegedly over privacy issues. His co-founder Brian Acton had left the year before to help establish Signal. Their earlier-than-scheduled departure cost them $1.3 billion. In September 2018, the founders of Instagram announced that they were leaving. One subsequently said, 'no one ever leaves a job because everything's awesome'.

Whatever the stock market success, this is a corporation in crisis, one which has had a hard time identifying forensically all of the areas in which it may be vulnerable because of historic and current corporate executive behaviour. Leaks have come from within the company on an unprecedented basis. Morale in Facebook had slumped. Staff were worried about public trust: 'It is a major concern and a major topic of conversation', said Richard Allan at the International Grand Committee hosted by the UK House of Commons in London in November 2018. Facebook listed a significant number of regulatory and legislative risks in its SEC filing in January 2019 which could restrict its business activities, including laws and regulations which 'can impose different obligations or be more restrictive than those in the United States'. Facebook's data problems were now under criminal investigation.[2]

The last three years have been a period when legislators in liberal democracies across the world have come to understand better the underlying business model – and business ethics – of this particular corporate expression of surveillance capitalism. Liberal democracies have been engaged in a process of building the necessary 'discursive capacity' to address the challenges of Big Tech. Problems have been identified and many solutions advanced. Some of those solutions are limited and specific to particular aspects of Facebook's behaviour. Others challenge their business model more deeply. As Facebook has become more exposed before legislatures and regulators worldwide, repeated examples of poor corporate practice have come to light, including a lack of transparency, an unwillingness to own problems until Facebook is about to be exposed by news organisations or about to give testimony to legislative committees and deliberate withholding of information. Meanwhile, legislators and regulators are co-operating across the world in an unprecedented way to deal with the challenge of this one company. The global interest in the UK House of Commons hearing with Cambridge Analytica whistleblower Christopher Wylie on 27 March 2018, which followed the joint reporting by the *Observer* in the UK and the *New York Times*, provided the biggest live-streamed audience the UK Parliament has ever had.

Facebook, for some, is now an empire.[3] But the fight-back has begun. We must fix Facebook. Facebook's leaders have demonstrated repeatedly that they cannot. Fixing Facebook will take coordinated international regulation. It will require scrutiny of its data-mining business model, as the German Bundeskartellamt has done. It will require analysis of its role in the digital advertising market, as the Australian Competition and Consumer Commission has commenced. It will require forensic analysis of its data practices, as the UK Information Commissioner has done in relation to Cambridge Analytica and political advertising. It will require interrogation of Facebook's recommendation and other algorithms, as the UK Government's Online Harms White Paper proposes. It will require personal obligations on Facebook's founder and other senior executives and directors, as one FTC commissioner has suggested. It will require re-designation of Facebook as a utility, as Senator Warren proposes. It will require breakup of the Facebook family of companies in a meaningful way, focusing as much on its vertically integrated advertising operation as on its ownership of Instagram, Messenger and WhatsApp. The planned integration of its family of companies should be blocked by regulators in the US and Europe. It will require restrictions on Facebook's ability to enter and operate in certain market segments. It necessitates limits on opportunities to collect and process and combine data from different sources and to infer what is being done by users and legally enforceable ethical limits on what Facebook can do with the data it currently holds, including behavioural nudges and emotional manipulation. It will require new taxation systems which reduce the incentives for corporate surveillance and support the development of independent media. It will demand modernised electoral laws around the world and a ban on dark money and dark advertising.

Facebook is already recognised as a national security issue in many countries. Its desire to move into cryptocurrency, based on an encrypted messaging platform, potentially threatens banking, stock market and currency exchange laws internationally.[4] Regulators need the powers to act to protect international financial systems from Facebook's imperial adventurism. We need to move fast and break up Facebook, before it breaks us.

Notes

1 *Companies like Facebook should not be allowed to behave like 'digital gangsters'*: House of Commons, 2019b; Eleanor Ainge Roy, Facebook Are Morally Bankrupt Liars Says New Zealand's Privacy Commissioner, *Guardian*, 8 April 2019, www.theguardian.com/technology/2019/apr/08/facebook-are-morally-bankrupt-liars-says-new-zealands-privacy-commissioner, and former FTC Director of Consumer Protection David Vladeck has said 'Facebook is now a serial offender', Facebook, Cambridge Analytica and the Regulator's Dilemma: Clueless or Venal? 4 April 2018, https://blog.harvardlawreview.org/facebook-cambridge-analytica-and-the-regulators-dilemma-clueless-or-venal/.

2 Jessi Hempel, Facebook Just Tapped the New Mark Zuckerberg, *Wired*, 12 May 2018, www.wired.com/story/facebook-just-tapped-the-next-mark-zuckerberg/; Sheera Frenkel, Nicholas Confessore, Cecilia Kang, Matthew Rosenberg and Jack Nicas, Delay, Deny, and Deflect: How Facebook's Leaders Fought Through Crisis, *New York Times*, 14 November 2018, www.nytimes.com/2018/11/14/technology/facebook-data-russia-election-racism.html; Gabriel J.X. Dance, Nicholas Confessore and Michael LaForgia, Facebook Gave Device Makers Deep Access to Data on Users and Friends, *New York Times*, 3 June 2018, www.nytimes.com/interactive/2018/06/03/technology/facebook-device-partners-users-friends-data.html; Gabriel J.X. Dance, Michael LaForgia and Nicholas Confessore, As Facebook Raised a Privacy Wall, It Carved an Opening for Tech Giants, *New York Times*, 18 December 2018, www.nytimes.com/2018/12/18/technology/facebook-privacy.html?action=click&module=RelatedCoverage&pgtype=Article&region=Footer; on the novelty of leaks, see Noah Kulwin, The Organic Side, to Me, Is Scarier Than the Ad Side, Antonio Garcia Marquez interview, *New York* magazine, April 2018, http://nymag.com/intelligencer/2018/04/antonio-garcia-martinez-former-facebook-employee-interview.html; on Facebook internal morale, see Richard Allan evidence to the International Grand Committee, November 2018, and for fully detailed background, Nicholas Thompson and Fred Vogelstein, 15 Months of Fresh Hell in Facebook, 16 April 2019, www.wired.com/story/facebook-mark-zuckerberg-15-months-of-fresh-hell/; SEC, Facebook Form 10-k Filing for 2018, www.sec.gov/Archives/edgar/data/1326801/000132680119000009/fb-12312018x10k.htm; Michael LaForgia, Matthew Rosenberg and Gabriel J.X. Dance, Facebook's Data Deals Are Under Criminal Investigation, *New York Times*, 13 March 2019, www.nytimes.com/2019/03/13/technology/facebook-data-deals-investigation.html.

3 Ellen P. Goodman and Julia Powles, Facebook and Google: Most Powerful and Secretive Empires We Have Ever Known, *Guardian*, 28 September 2018, www.theguardian.com/technology/2016/sep/28/google-facebook-powerful-secretive-empire-transparency; Zuckerberg Now Runs Not a Business but an Empire: It's Time to Strike Back, Business Leader, *Observer*, 30 September 2018, www.theguardian.com/technology/2018/sep/30/facebook-zuckerberg-empire-instagram-whatsapp-antitrust.

4 Alex Heath, Facebook's Blockchain Group Is on a Hiring Spree to Reinvent Money, *Cheddar*, 14 December 2018, https://medium.com/cheddar/facebooks-blockchain-group-is-on-a-hiring-spree-to-reinvent-money-30439db29f33; Sarah Frier and Julia Verhage, Facebook Is Developing a Cryptocurrency for WhatsApp Transfers, Sources Say, *Bloomberg*, 21 December 2018, www.bloomberg.com/news/articles/2018-12-21/facebook-is-said-to-develop-stablecoin-for-whatsapp-transfers.

Select bibliography

A more comprehensive bibliography of academic and legal sources consulted can be found online at www.routledge.com/9781138608979

ACCC. 2018. *Digital Platforms Inquiry: Preliminary Report*. Australian Competition and Consumer Commission.

Andrews, L. 2019. Public Administration, Public Leadership and the Construction of Public Value in the Age of the Algorithm and 'Big Data'. *Public Administration* 97(2), 296–310.

Bakir, V., and McStay, A. 2018. Fake News and the Economy of Emotions: Problems, Causes, Solutions. *Digital Journalism* 6(2).

Bakshy, E. et al. 2015. Exposure to Ideologically Diverse News and Opinion on Facebook. *Science* 348(6239), 1130–1132.

Baldwin, T. 2018. *Ctrl Alt Delete: How Politics and the Media Crashed Our Democracy*. London: C. Hurst & Co.

Baldwin-Philippi, J. 2017. The Myths of Data-Driven Campaigning. *Political Communication* 34(4), 627–633.

Bartlett, J. 2018. *The People vs Tech: How the Internet Is Killing Democracy (and How We Save It)*. London: Penguin Random House.

Barwise, P. 2018. Why Tech Markets Are Winner Take All. In Mair, J. et al. eds., *Anti-Social Media*. Bury St Edmunds: Abramis.

Barwise, P., and Watkins, S. 2018. The Evolution of Digital Dominance: How and Why We Got to GAFA. In Moore, M., and Tambini, D. eds., *Digital Dominance: The Power of Google, Amazon, Facebook, and Apple*. New York: Oxford University Press.

Benkler, Y. et al. 2018. *Network Propaganda: Manipulation, Disinformation, and Radicalization in American Politics*. New York: Oxford University Press.

Berlin, L. 2017. *Troublemakers: How a Generation of Silicon Valley Upstarts Invented the Future*. London: Simon & Schuster UK Ltd.

Bond, R., Fariss, C.J., Jones, J.J., Kramer, A.D.I., Marlow, C., Settle, J., and Fowler, J.H. 2012. 'A 61-Million Person Experiment in Social Mobilisation and Political Influence' [Research Letter]. *Nature*, 489, 295–298.

Borins, S.F., and Herst, B. 2018. *Negotiating Business Narratives: Fables of the Information Technology, Automobile Manufacturing, and Financial Trading Industries*. Cham: Palgrave Macmillan.

boyd, d. 2014. *It's Complicated*. New Haven: Yale University Press.

Bucher, T. 2012. Want to Be on the Top? Algorithmic Power and the Threat of Invisibility on Facebook. *New Media and Society* 14(7).

Bucher, T. 2018. *If . . . Then: Algorithmic Power and Politics*. New York: Oxford University Press.

Bundeskartellamt. 2019. *Bundeskartellamt Prohibits Facebook from Combining Data from Different Sources*, 7 February.

Cairncross, F. 2019. *The Cairncross Review: A Sustainable Future for Journalism*. London: DCMS.

Campbell, A. 2018. *Diaries Volume 7: From Crash to Defeat*. London: Biteback.

Caplan, R. 2018. Content or Context Moderation? *Data and Society*, 14 November. https://datasociety.net/output/content-or-context-moderation/.

Cerf, V. 2012. Dynamics of Disruptive Innovations. *Journal on Telecommunications and High Technology Law* 10.

Chang, E. 2018. *Brotopia*. New York: Penguin.

Colangelo, G., and Maggiolino, M. 2018. Data Accumulation and the Privacy–Antitrust Interface: Insights from the Facebook Case. *International Data Privacy Law* 8(3).

Cohen, N. 2017. *The Know-It-Alls: The Rise of Silicon Valley as a Political Powerhouse and Social Wrecking Ball*. New York: The New Press.

Comey, J. 2018. *A Higher Loyalty*. London: Macmillan.

Committee on Standards in Public Life. 2017. *Intimidation in Public Life*. Notes of Meeting with Facebook.

Data Protection Commissioner. 2011. *Facebook Ireland Ltd – Report of Audit*, 21 December.

Data Protection Commissioner. 2018. Annual Report.

DCMS. 2019. Online Harms White Paper.

Dotson, T. 2015. Technological Determinism and Permissionless Innovation as Technocratic Governing Mentalities: Psychocultural Barriers to the Democratization of Technology. *Engaging Science, Technology, and Society* 1.

EC. 2017. *Mergers: Commission Fines Facebook €110 Million for Providing Misleading Information About WhatsApp Takeover*. European Commission.

EC. 2018. *A Multi-Dimensional Approach to Disinformation*. Report of the independent high-level group on fake news and disinformation. European Commission.

EC. 2019. *Shaping Competition Policy in the Era of Digitisation*, 4 April.

Edwards, L. 2004. The Problem with Privacy. *International Review of Law Computers & Technology* 18(3).

Electoral Commission. 2018. Vote Leave Fined and Referred to the Police for Breaking Electoral Law, 17 July, www.electoralcommission.org.uk/i-am-a/jour nalist/electoral-commission-media-centre/party-and-election-finance-to-keep/ vote-leave-fined-and-referred-to-the-police-for-breaking-electoral-law.

Ezrachi, A., and Stucke, M.E. 2016. *Virtual Competition: The Promise and Perils of the Algorithm-Driven Economy*. Cambridge, MA: Harvard University Press.

Fattal, A. 2012. Facebook: Corporate Hackers, a Billion Users, and the Geo-Politics of the 'Social Graph'. *Anthropological Quarterly* 85(3).

Ferrary, M., and Gravenetter, M. 2009. The Role of Venture Capital Firms in Silicon Valley's Complex Innovation Network. *Economy and Society* 38(2).

Foer, F. 2017. *World Without Mind: The Existential Threat of Big Tech*. New York: Penguin Press.

Fogg, B.J. 2003. *Persuasive Technology: Using Computers to Change What We Think and Do*. Amsterdam and Boston: Morgan Kaufmann Publishers.

Foster, R. 2012. *News Plurality in a Digital World*. Oxford: Reuters Institute for the Study of Journalism.

FTC. 2011. *Facebook Settles FTC Charges That It Deceived Consumers by Failing to Keep Privacy Promises*. Federal Trade Commission.

FTC. 2012. *Statement of the Commission*. Federal Trade Commission.

FTC. 2014. *Letter to Facebook and Instagram*, 10 April. Federal Trade Commission.

Furman, J. 2019. *Unlocking Digital Competition: Report of the Digital Competition Expert Panel*. HM Treasury.

Gallagher, B. 2018. *How to Turn Down a Billion Dollars: The Snapchat Story*. New York: St. Martin's Press.

Galloway, S. 2017. *The Four: The Hidden DNA of Amazon, Apple, Facebook, and Google*. New York: Portfolio, Penguin.

Gerlitz, C., and Helmond, A. 2013. The Like Economy: Social Buttons and the Data-Intensive Web. *New Media & Society* 15(8).

Gillespie, T. 2018. *Custodians of the Internet: Platforms, Content Moderation, and the Hidden Decisions That Shape Social Media*. New Haven: Yale University Press.

Goggin, G. 2014. Facebook's Mobile Career. *New Media & Society* 16(7).

Golumbia, D. 2014. 'Permissionless Innovation': Using Technology to Dismantle the Republic. www.uncomputing.org/?p=1383.

Graef, I. 2018. When Data Evolves into Market Power: Data Concentration and Data Abuse Under Competition Law. In Moore, M., and Tambini, D. eds., *Digital Dominance*. Oxford: Oxford University Press.

Greenfield, S. 2015. *Mind Change*. London: Penguin.

Habermas, J. 2006. Political Communication in Media Society: Does Democracy Still Enjoy an Epistemic Dimension? The Impact of Normative Theory on Empirical Research. *Communication Theory* 16(4).

Heclo, H. 1974. *Modern Social Politics in Britain and Sweden: From Relief to Income Maintenance*. New Haven: Yale University Press.

Helberger, N., Borgesius, F.Z., and Reyna, A. 2017. The Perfect Match? A Closer Look at the Relationship Between EU Consumer Law and Data Protection Law. *Common Market Law Review* 54(5).

Hindman, M. 2018. *The Internet Trap*. Princeton: Princeton University Press.

Honeycutt, C., and Cunliffe, D. 2010. The Use of the Welsh Language on Facebook: An Initial Investigation. *Information, Communication & Society* 13(2).

House of Commons. 2017. *Hate Crime: Hate, Abuse and Extremism Online*. 14th Report, Home Affairs Committee, 17 March.

House of Commons. 2018a. *Disinformation and Fake News*. Interim Report, 5th Report, Digital, Culture, Media and Sport Committee, 29 July.

House of Commons. 2018b. *Note by Chair and Selected Documents Ordered from Six4Three*. Digital, Culture, Media and Sport Committee, 5 December.

House of Commons. 2019a. *Impact of Social Media and Screen Use on Young People's Health*. Science and Technology Committee, 31 January.

House of Commons. 2019b. *Disinformation and Fake News*. Final Report, 8th Report, Digital, Culture, Media and Sport Committee, 7 February.

House of Commons. 2019c. *Oral Evidence*. Home Affairs Committee, 25 April.

House of Lords. 2018a. AI in the UK – Ready, Willing, and Able? Select Committee on Artificial Intelligence, 16 April.

House of Lords. 2018b. UK Advertising in a Digital Age. Communications Committee, 11 April.

House of Lords. 2019. The Internet – to Regulate or Not to Regulate? Communications Committee, 9 March.

Howard, P. 2018. *Subject Matter: Impact of Unlawful Overspending on Digital Advertising by Vote Leave and BeLeave Campaigns in the 2016 EU Referendum*. Oxford Internet Institute, 30 November.

Howells, R. 2015. *Journey to the Centre of a News Black Hole: Examining the Democratic Deficit in a Town with No Newspaper* (Doctoral dissertation, Cardiff University).

Information Commissioner's Office. 2018a. *Investigation into Data Analytics for Political Purposes: Update*, 11 July.

Information Commissioner's Office. 2018b. *Democracy Disrupted?* 11 July.

Information Commissioner's Office. 2018c. *Investigation into Data Analytics for Political Purposes: Action We've Taken*, 6 November.

Information Commissioner's Office. 2018d. *Facebook Ireland Monetary Penalty Notice*, 25 October.

Information Commissioner's Office. 2019. *ICO Launches Consultation on Code of Practice to Help Protect Children Online*, 12 April.

International Grand Committee. 2018. *Oral Evidence Taken Before the International Digital Culture Media and Sport Grand Committee*, 27 November.

Iosifidis, P., and Andrews, L. 2019. Regulating the Internet Intermediaries in a Post-Truth World: Beyond Media Policy? *International Communication Gazette*.

Jamieson, K. 2018. *Cyber War*. Oxford: Oxford University Press.

John, N.A. 2013. Sharing and Web 2.0: The Emergence of a Keyword. *New Media & Society* 15(2), 167–182.

Jones, J.J., Bond, R.M., Bakshy, E., Eckles, D., and Fowler, J.H. 2017. Social Influence and Political Mobilization: Further Evidence from a Randomized Experiment in the 2012 U.S. Presidential Election. *PLOS One* 12(4), 1–9.

Jørgensen, R.F. 2018. Framing Human Rights: Exploring Storytelling Within Internet Companies. *Information, Communication & Society* 21(3).

Karpf, D. 2017. Digital Politics After Trump. *Annals of the International Communication Association* 41(2).

Katz, E., Lazarsfeld, P.F., and Roper, E. 2017. *Personal Influence: The Part Played by People in the Flow of Mass Communications*. London: Routledge.

Khan, L. 2018. Sources of Tech Platform Power. *Georgetown Law Technology Review* 2(325).

Kim, Y.M. et al. 2018. The Stealth Media? Groups and Targets Behind Divisive Issue Campaigns on Facebook. *Political Communication* 35(4).

Kingdon, J. 1984. *Agendas, Alternatives, and Public Policies*. London: Longman.

Kirkpatrick, D. 2011. *The Facebook Effect: The Inside Story of the Company That Is Connecting the World*. New York: Simon & Schuster Paperbacks.

Kohl, U. 2012. 'The Rise and Rise of Online Intermediaries in the Governance of the Internet and Beyond – Connectivity Intermediaries'. *International Review of Law, Computers and Technology* 26(2–3), 185–210.

Kosinski, M., Stillwell, D., and Graepel, T. 2013. Digital Records of Behavior Expose Personal Traits. *Proceedings of the National Academy of Sciences* 110(15), April.

Kramer, A.D., Guillory, J.E., and Hancock, J.T. 2014. Experimental Evidence of Massive-Scale Emotional Contagion Through Social Networks. *Proceedings of the National Academy of Sciences* 111(24).

Kreiss, D. 2017. Micro-Targeting, the Quantified Persuasion. *Internet Policy Review* 6(4).

Kreiss, D. 2018. The Networked Self in the Age of Identity Fundamentalism. in: Papacharissi, Z. ed. *A Networked Self and Platforms, Stories, Connections*. New York: Routledge, Taylor & Francis Group

Kreiss, D., and Mcgregor, S.C. 2018. Technology Firms Shape Political Communication: The Work of Microsoft, Facebook, Twitter, and Google with Campaigns During the 2016 U.S. Presidential Cycle. *Political Communication* 35(2).

Kreiss, D., et al. 2018. In Their Own Words: Political Practitioner Accounts of Candidates, Audiences, Affordances, Genres, and Timing in Strategic Social Media Use. *Political Communication* 35(1).

Lewis, R., and Marwick, A. 2017. 'Taking the Red Pill: Ideological Motivations for Spreading Online Disinformation.' Understanding and Addressing the Disinformation Ecosystem, University of Pennsylvania Annenberg School for Communication, Philadelphia, PA, Lewis, December 15–16.

Livingstone, S. 2018. Children: A Special Case for Privacy? *Intermedia* 46(2).

Losse, K. 2012. *The Boy Kings: A Journey into the Heart of the Social Network*. First Free Press. New York: Free Press.

Lynskey, O. 2018. The Power of Providence: The Role of Platforms in Leveraging the Legibility of Users to Accentuate Inequality. In Moore, M., and Tambini, D. eds., *Digital Dominance: The Power of Google, Amazon, Facebook, and Apple*. New York: Oxford University Press.

Margetts, H. et al. 2016. *Political Turbulence: How Social Media Shape Collective Action*. Princeton, NJ: Princeton University Press.

Martinez, A. 2016. *Chaos Monkeys*. New York: HarperCollins.

Marwick, A.E. 2013. *Status Update: Celebrity, Publicity, and Branding in the Social Media Age*. New Haven: Yale University Press.

Marwick, A.E. 2018. Why Do People Share Fake News? A Sociotechnical Model of Media Effects. *Georgetown Law Technology Review* 474.

Marwick, A.E., and boyd, d. 2014. Networked Privacy: How Teenagers Negotiate Context in Social Media. *New Media & Society* 16(7).

McNair, B. 2018. *Fake News*. London: Routledge.

McNamee, R. 2019. *Zucked*. London: HarperCollins.

Mezrich, B. 2009. *The Accidental Billionaires*. New York: Doubleday.

Moore, M. 2018. *Democracy Hacked: Political Turmoil and Information Warfare in the Digital Age*. London: Oneworld.

Moore, M., and Tambini, D. eds. 2018. *Digital Dominance: The Power of Google, Amazon, Facebook, and Apple*. New York: Oxford University Press.

Mulligan, D.K., and Griffin, D.S., 2018. Rescripting Search to Respect the Right to Truth, *Georgetown Law Technology Review* 2(2), 557.

Nairn, A. 2018. Legal, Decent, Honest, Truthful . . . and Trustworthy? In Mair, J. et al. eds., *Anti-Social Media*. Bury St Edmunds: Abramis.

Napoli, P., and Caplan, R. 2017. Why Media Companies Insist They're Not Media Companies, Why They're Wrong, and Why It Matters. *First Monday* 22(5).

Nieborg, D.B., and Helmond, A. 2019. The Political Economy of Facebook's Platformization in the Mobile Ecosystem: Facebook Messenger as a Platform Instance. *Media, Culture & Society* 41(2), 196–218.

Nielsen, R.K. 2018. *The Changing Economic Contexts of Journalism*. Draft chapter for the second edition of the ICA Handbook of Journalism Studies, edited by Karin Wahl-Jorgensen and Thomas Hanitzsch. London: Routledge.

Nielsen, R.K., and Ganter, S.A. 2018. Dealing with Digital Intermediaries: A Case Study of the Relations Between Publishers and Platforms. *New Media & Society* 20(4).

OECD. 2016. *Big Data – Bringing Competition Policy to the Digital Era*, Background note by the Secretariat, 29–30 November.

OFT. 2012. *Anticipated Acquisition by Facebook Inc of Instagram Inc ME/5525/12*, Office of Fair Trading, 22 August.

Orben, A., and Przybylski, A.K. 2019. The Association Between Adolescent Well-Being and Digital Technology Use. *Nature Human Behaviour* 3.

Owen, T. 2015. *Disruptive Power: The Crisis of the State in the Digital Age*. Oxford: Oxford University Press.

Pai, H.-H. 2016. *Angry White People: Coming Face-to-Face with the British Far Right*. London: Zed Books.

Papacharissi, Z. 2010. *A Private Sphere: Democracy in a Digital Age*. Cambridge and Malden, MA: Polity.

Papacharissi, Z. ed. 2011. *A Networked Self: Identity, Community and Culture on Social Network Sites*. New York: Routledge.

Papacharissi, Z. 2015. *Affective Publics: Sentiment, Technology, and Politics*. Oxford and New York: Oxford University Press.

Papacharissi, Z. ed. 2018a. *A Networked Self and Human Augmentics, Artificial Intelligence, Sentience*. New York: Routledge, Taylor & Francis Group.

Papacharissi, Z. ed. 2018b. *A Networked Self and Platforms, Stories, Connections*. New York: Routledge.

Pariser, E. 2011. *The Filter Bubble: What the Internet Is Hiding from You*. New York: Penguin Press.

Pasquale, F. 2015. *The Black Box Society: The Secret Algorithms That Control Money and Information*. Cambridge: Harvard University Press.

Pasquale, F. 2017. From Territorial to Functional Sovereignty: The Case of Amazon. https://lpeblog.org/2017/12/06/from-territorial-to-functional-sovereignty-the-case-of-amazon/.

Patrick, J. 2017. *Alternative War*. Buckinghamshire, UK: Cynefin Books.

Phillips, W. 2013. The House That Fox Built: Anonymous, Spectacle, and Cycles of Amplification. *Television & New Media* 14(6).

Potter, D. 1996. *Karaoke and Cold Lazarus*. London: Faber.

Privacy Commissioner of Canada. 2009. Report of Findings into the Complaint Filed by the Canadian Internet Policy and Public Interest Clinic (CIPPIC) Against Facebook Inc, 16 July.

Privacy Commissioner of Canada. 2019. *Facebook Refuses to Address Serious Privacy Deficiencies Despite Public Apologies for 'Breach of Trust'*, 25 April.

Rahman, K.S. 2018a. The New Utilities: Private Power, Social Infrastructure, and the Revival of the Public Utility Concept. *Cardozo Law Review* 39(5).

Rahman, K.S. 2018b. Regulating Informational Infrastructure: Internet Platforms as the New Public Utilities. *Georgetown Law Technology Review* 2(234).

Sadowski, J. 2019. When Data Is Capital: Datafication, Accumulation, and Extraction. *Big Data & Society*.

SEC. 2012. *Facebook Inc*. Registration Statement. Securities and Exchanges Commission.

Shirky, C. 2008. *Here Comes Everybody: The Power of Organizing Without Organizations*. New York: Penguin Press.

Simanowski, R. 2018. *Facebook Society: Losing Ourselves in Sharing Ourselves*. New York: Columbia University Press.

Spar, D. 2001. *Riding the Waves*. Orlando: Harcourt.

Special Counsel. 2018. *Indictment*, 16 February.

Srinivasan, D. 2019. The Antitrust Case Against Facebook: A Monopolist's Journey Towards Pervasive Surveillance in Spite of Consumers' Preference for Privacy. *Berkeley Business Law Journal* 16(39).

Srnicek, N. 2017. *Platform Capitalism*. Cambridge and Malden, MA: Polity.

Streeter, T. 1999. 'That Deep Romantic Chasm'; Libertarianism, Neoliberalism and the Computer Culture. In Calabrese, A., and Bargeman, J.-C. eds., *Communications Citizenship and Social Policy*. Rowman & Littlefield.

Stucke, M.E., and Grunes, A.P. 2016. *Big Data and Competition Policy*. Oxford: Oxford University Press.

Sunstein, C. 2017. *Republic 2.0*. Princeton: Princeton University Press.

Tambini, D. 2018. Social Media Power and Election Legitimacy. In Moore, M., and Tambini, D. eds., *Digital Dominance*. Oxford: Oxford University Press.

Taplin, J.T. 2017. *Move Fast and Break Things: How Facebook, Google, and Amazon Cornered Culture and Undermined Democracy*. New York: Little, Brown and Company.

Thiel, P.A., and Masters, B. 2014. *Zero to One: Notes on Startups, or How to Build the Future*. New York: Crown Business.

Thompson, M. 2018. Journalism, Free Speech and the Search and Social Giants. In Mair, J. et al. eds., *Anti-Social Media*. Bury St Edmunds: Abramis.

Toff, B., and Nielsen, R.K. 2018. 'I Just Google It': Folk Theories of Distributed Discovery. *Journal of Communication* 68(3).

Tufekci, Z. 2008. Grooming, Gossip, Facebook and Myspace: What Can We Learn About These Sites from Those Who Won't Assimilate? *Information, Communication & Society* 11(4).

Tufekci, Z. 2010. Google Buzz: The Corporatization of Social Commons, February. http://technosociology.org/?p=102.

Tufekci, Z. 2014. Engineering the Public: Big Data, Surveillance and Computational Politics. *First Monday* 19(7).

Tufekci, Z. 2015. Algorithmic Harms Beyond Facebook and Google: Emergent Challenges of Computational Agency. *Colorado Technology Law Journal* 13(2).

Tufekci, Z. 2017. *Twitter and Tear Gas: The Power and Fragility of Networked Protest.* New Haven and London: Yale University Press.

Turner, F. 2006. *From Counter Culture to Cyber Culture.* Chicago: The University of Chicago Press.

Turow, J. 2011. *The Daily You: How the New Advertising Industry Is Defining Your Identity and Your Worth.* New Haven: Yale University Press.

UK CMOs. 2019. *UK CMO Commentary on Screen Time and Social Media Map of Reviews,* 7 February.

US Senate. 2018. *Putin's Asymmetric Assault on Democracy in Russia and Europe: Implications for U.S. National Security.* Minority Staff Report, Foreign Affairs Committee.

Vaidhyanathan, S. 2018. *Antisocial Media: How Facebook Disconnects US and Undermines Democracy.* New York: Oxford University Press.

van Dijck, J. 2013. *The Culture of Connectivity.* New York: Oxford University Press.

van Dijck, J. et al. 2018. *The Platform Society.* New York: Oxford University Press.

Wagner, B. 2018. Dominant Internet Intermediaries as Arbiters of Internet Speech. In Moore, M., and Tambini, D. eds., *Digital Dominance.* Oxford: Oxford University Press.

Wahl-Jorgensen, K. 2018a. The Emotional Architecture of Social Media. In Papacharissi, Z. ed., *A Networked Self and Platforms, Stories, Connections.* London: Routledge.

Wahl-Jorgensen, K. 2018b. *Emotions, Media and Politics.* Cambridge: Polity Press.

Wardle, C. 2018. The Need for Smarter Definitions and Practical, Timely Empirical Research on Information Disorder. *Digital Journalism* 6(8).

Wardle, C., and Derakhshan, H. 2017. *Information Disorder: Toward an Interdisciplinary Framework for Research and Policy Making.* Council of Europe Report, DGI, 9.

Washington Post. 2018a. Transcript of Mark Zuckerberg's Senate Hearing, 10 April. www.washingtonpost.com/news/the-switch/wp/2018/04/10/transcript-of-mark-zucker bergs-senate-hearing/?utm_term=.769519dbf99b.

Washington Post. 2018b. Transcript of Zuckerberg's Appearance Before House Committee. www.washingtonpost.com/news/the-switch/wp/2018/04/11/transcript-of-zuckerbergs-appearance-before-house-committee/?utm_term=.7f93c59bf5dc.

White House. 2016. 'Remarks by the President in Opening Remarks and Panel Discussion at White House Frontiers Conference' Office of the Press Secretary. *The White House,* 13 October. www.whitehouse.gov/the-press-office/2016/10/13/ remarks-president-opening-remarks-and-panel-discussion-white-house.

Williams, R. 1961. *The Long Revolution.* Harmondsworth: Penguin.

Williams, R. 1974. *Television, Technology and Cultural Form.* London: Fontana.

Williams, R. 1983. *Towards 2000.* London: Penguin.

Williams, R. 1989. *On Television.* London: Routledge.

Winner, L. 1997. Cyberlibertarian Myths and the Prospects for Community. *ACM SIGCAS Computers and Society* 27(3).

Wu, T. 2016. *The Attention Merchants: The Epic Scramble to Get Inside Our Heads*. New York: Alfred A. Knopf.

Wu, T. 2018. *The Curse of Bigness: Antitrust in the New Gilded Age*. New York: Columbia Global Reports.

Yeung, K. 2017. 'Hypernudge': Big Data as a Mode of Regulation by Design. *Information, Communication & Society* 20(1), 118–136.

Youyou, W., Kosinski, M., and Stilwell, D. 2015. Computer-Based Personality Judgements Are More Accurate Than Those Made by Humans. *Proceedings of the National Academy of Sciences* 112(4).

Zuboff, S. 2015. Big Other: Surveillance Capitalism and the Prospects of an Information Civilization. *Journal of Information Technology* 30(1).

Zuboff, S. 2019. *The Age of Surveillance Capitalism*. London: Profile Books.

Zuckerberg, D. 2018. *Not All Dead White Men: Classics and Misogyny in the Digital Age*. Cambridge, MA: Harvard University Press.

Zuckerberg, R. 2013. *Dot Complicated*. New York: HarperCollins.

Index

Action, Brian 109
Albright, Jonathan 64, 77
Allan, Richard 109
Andreessen, Marc 2, 17
Angus, Charlie 11

Bakir, Vian 62
Bannon, Steve 65, 75
Barlow, John Perry 16
Bell, Emily 58
Benkler, Yochai 65
Bezos, Jeff 15
Bosworth, Andrew 81
boyd, danah 40, 48, 50
Brand, Stewart 14
Brown, Michael 63

Cadwalladr, Carole 15, 44
Cairncross, Frances 57, 66, 67, 97
Caplan, Robyn 101
Carr, John 49, 102
Cerf, Vincent 18
Chan, Priscilla 17
Chang, Emily 15
Clegg, Nick 102
Clinton, Hillary 32, 64, 75
Collins, Damian 75
Comey, James 83
Cox, Chris 109
Cruz, Ted 44
Cummings, Dominic 76

Denham, Elizabeth 45
Derakhshan, Hossein 62
Dick, Jose van 64
DiResta, Renee 50, 78

Edwards, Lilian 103

Feld, Harold 97
Foer, Franklin 103
Foster, Robin 96
Furman, Jason 97

Ganter, Susan 57
Ghonim, Wael 32, 33, 34
Gillespie, Tarleton 60, 92, 99, 100
Grassegger, Hannes 32
Griffiths, Chris 31
Grunes, Allen 5

Hammond, Philip 103
Harris, Tristan 48
Helberger, Natali 60
Hieatt, Clare 24
Hieatt, David 24, 25
Hindman, Matthew 95
Hoffman, Reid 2
Howells, Rachel 59

James, Margot 80
Jamieson, Kathleen Hall 75
Jobbins, Sion 31
Jobs, Steve 14
Jones, Robert 30

Katz, Elihu 63, 64
Khan, Lina 103
Kogan, Aleksandr 43, 44
Kosinski, Michael 44
Koum, Jan 109
Krebs, Brian 46
Kreiss, Daniel 79

Lazarsfeld, Paul 63, 64
Lessig, Larry 18
Lewis, Rebecca 80
Livingstone, Sonia 49
Losse, Kate 15, 16, 18, 45, 46
Lucas, Ian 74
Luckie, Mark S. 16

Mackey, Stephen 30
Markle, Meghan 25
Martinez, Antonio Garcia 48
Marwick, Alice 12, 40, 64, 80
McNamee, Roger 4, 48, 75, 94
McStay, Andrew 62
Moore, Martin 19, 64, 79, 92
Morales, Oscar 32
Mueller, Robert 74, 77
Musk, Elon 15

Nielsen, Rasmus Kleis 57

Obama, Barack 19, 76, 83, 103
Obama, Michelle 16
Owen, Taylor 58

Palihapitiya, Chamath 19
Papacharissi, Zizi 11, 28, 33, 39
Parker, Sean 1
Pasquale, Frank 16
Piechota, Greg 58
Pincus, Mark 2
Potter, Dennis 14
Putin, Vladimir 77

Rand, Ayn 18
Reynolds, Matt 101
Richards, Ed 94
Russell, Molly 50

Said, Khaled 33
Sandberg, Sheryl: credited for turning
    around Facebook culture, *Lean-In*
    book, criticised by Michelle Obama
    16; employs Elliott Schrage 13; hired
    by Zuckerberg 4; on small businesses
    and Facebook 27; tensions with
    Zuckerberg 109
Schrage, Elliott 13
Schrage, Michael 13
Shirky, Clay 31

Simanowksi, Roberto 34
Sontag, Susan 28
Sorkin, Aaron 18
Soros, George 109
Srinavasan, Dina 5
Stamos, Alex 80, 109
Streeter, Thomas 11
Streeting, Wes 31
Stucke, Maurice 5
Sunstein, Cass 50, 63, 93, 99
Swisher, Kara 17

Tambini, Damian 93, 98
Taplin, Jonathan 18
Thiel, Peter 2, 15, 17, 19
Thompson, Mark 58, 62
Trump, Donald 75
Tufekci, Zeynep 27, 28, 33, 63
Turow, Joseph 13

Vaidhyanathan, Siva 17, 28, 39, 97

Wagner, Ben 100, 102
Wahl-Jorgensen, Karin 40
Walbey, Helen 25, 26, 27
Walbey, Stephen 25
Wardle, Claire 62
Warner, Mark 95
Warren, Elizabeth 95, 110
Watson, Tom 13
Williams, Joy 11
Williams, Raymond 11, 12, 18, 33, 39
Wu, Timothy 5, 17, 4
Wylie, Christopher 44, 110

Yeung, Karen 46

Zimmer, Bob 13
Zuboff, Shoshana 13
Zuckerberg, Donna 79
Zuckerberg, Mark: 2019 strategy
    7; able to delete his Facebook
    messages 29; on ability to see
    Facebook users' data 46; admits
    Facebook algorithm prioritises
    polarising and extreme posts 49,
    50; in advertisements promising to
    protect user data 24; on Cambridge
    Analytica and Kogan 44, 45;
    connectivity as human right 81;

early investments, development of News Feed 2; Facebook effect on 2016 US Presidential election, Gizmodo expose 65; Facebook as 'living database', Senate questioning 13; Facebook as platform, rivalry with Google 3; Facebook as 'the best personalised newspaper' 60; Facebook election influence globally 74; Facebook's origin 1; in favour of regulation 92; Founder, Master and Commander, Facebook like a government 16; GDPR as global standard, Facebook as utility 94; on ideology of Silicon Valley 14; importance of Facebook Groups, charity efforts, Egyptian uprising 32; IPO letter, privileging of engineers 18; knowledge of Russian disinformation threat 77; 'not really familiar' with Palantir 19; problems with Beacon, hires Sandberg, IPO 4; rows back on government analogy, control of company, 'presidential' tour of USA 17; on selling data, Facebook advertising 41; on shadow or dark profiles 45; Six4Three emails and Vine, privacy 'pivot' 6, 82; tensions with Sandberg 109; vagueness in Congress 42